EYEWITNESS TRAVEL
ITALIAN
VISUAL
PHRASE BOOK

A Dorling Kindersley Book

LONDON, NEW YORK, MELBOURNE,
MUNICH, DELHI

Senior Editor Angela Wilkes
Art Editor Silke Spingies
Production Editor Lucy Baker
Production Controller Inderjit Bhullar
Managing Editor Julie Oughton
Managing Art Editor Christine Keilty
Reference Publisher Jonathan Metcalf
Art Director Bryn Walls

Produced for Dorling Kindersley by
SP Creative Design
Editor Heather Thomas
Designer Rolando Ugolino

Language content for Dorling Kindersley
by First Edition Translations Ltd,
Cambridge, UK
Translator Esmeralda Lines
Editor Gabriella Barra
Typesetting Essential Typesetting

First published in Great Britain in 2008
by Dorling Kindersley Limited,
80 Strand, London WC2R 0RL

A Penguin Company

2 4 6 8 10 9 7 5 3 1

A CIP catalogue record for this book is
available from the British Library

ISBN: 978-1-4053-3108-1

Printed by Leo Paper China

Discover more at
www.dk.com

CONTENTS

INTRODUCTION

This book provides all the key words and phrases you are
likely to need in everyday situations. It is grouped into
themes, and key phrases are broken down into short
sections, to help you build a wide variety of sentences.
A lot of the vocabulary is illustrated to make it easy to
remember, and "You may hear" boxes feature questions
you are likely to hear. At the back of the book there is a
menu guide, listing about 500 food terms, and a 2,000-
word two-way dictionary. Numbers and the most useful
phrases are listed on the jacket flaps for quick reference.

Nouns

All Italian nouns (words for things, people, and ideas) are
masculine or feminine. The gender of singular nouns is
usually shown by the word for "the": **il** or **lo** (masculine)
and **la** (feminine). They change to **l'** before vowels. The
plural forms are **i** or **gli** (masculine) and **le** (feminine).

Adjectives

Most Italian adjectives change endings according to
whether they describe a masculine or feminine, singular or
plural word. In this book the singular masculine form is
shown, followed by the alternative feminine ending:

I'm lost   **Mi sono perso/a**

"You"

There are two ways of saying "you" in Italian: **lei** (polite)
and **tu** (familiar). In this book we have used **lei**
throughout, as that is what you normally use with people
you don't know.

Verbs

Verbs change according to whether they are in the singular
or plural. In phrases where this happens, the singular form
of the verb is followed by the plural form:

Where is/are…?   **Dov'è/Dove sono…?**

Pronunciation guide

Below each Italian word or phrase in this book, you will find a pronunciation guide in italics. Read it as if it were English and you should be understood, but remember that it is only a guide and for the best results you should listen to and mimic native speakers. Some Italian sounds are different from those in English, so take note of how the letters below are pronounced.

a	like a in car
ai	like i in mile
ao, au	like ow in cow
c	before a, o, and u, like k in kite
	before i and e, like ch in church
cc	like ch in church
ch	like k in keep
e	like e in pet
ei	like ay in day
g	before a, o, and u, like g in get
	before i and e, like j in jam
gh	like g in got
gli	like lli in million
gn	like ni in onion
h	silent
i	like ee in keep
o	like o in pot
oi	like oy in boy
qu	like qu in quick
r	rolled
s	like s in see or z in zoo
sc	before a, o, and u, like sk in skip
	before i or e, like sh in ship
u	like oo in boot
z	like ts in pets, or ds in loads

ESSENTIALS

In this section, you will find the essential words
and useful phrases you need for basic everyday
talk and situations. Be aware of cultural differences
when you're addressing Italian people, and also
remember that they tend to be quite formal
when they are greeting each other, using *signore*
(for men), *signora* (for women) and *signorina*
(for girls and younger women). These titles are
also used with surnames.

GREETINGS

Hello	Salve *salveh*
Good evening	Buonasera *bwonaserah*
Good night	Buonanotte *bwonanotteh*
Goodbye	Arrivederci *arreevederchee*
Hi/bye!	Ciao/ciao! *chow*
Pleased to meet you	Piacere *pyachereh*
How are you?	Come sta? *komeh stah*
Fine, thanks	Bene, grazie *beneh gratsye*
You're welcome	Prego *pregoh*
My name is…	Mi chiamo… *mee kyamoh*
What's your name?	Come si chiama? *komeh see kyamah*
What's his/her name?	Lui/lei come si chiama? *looee/lay komeh see kyamah*
This is…	Questo/a è… *kwestoh/ah eh*
Nice to meet you	Lieto/a di conoscerla *lyetoh/ah dee konosherlah*
See you tomorrow	A domani *ah domanee*
See you soon	A presto *ah prestoh*

SMALL TALK

Yes/no	Sì/no *see/noh*
Please	Per favore *pehr favoreh*
Thank you (very much)	(Molte) grazie *(molteh) gratsye*
You're welcome	Prego *pregoh*
OK/fine	OK/bene *okay/beneh*
Pardon?	Scusi? *skoozee*
Excuse me	Mi scusi *mee skoozee*
Sorry	Mi dispiace *mee deespyacheh*
I don't know	Non so *non soh*
I don't understand	Non capisco *non kapeeskoh*
Could you repeat that?	Può ripetere? *pwo reepetereh*
I don't speak Italian	Non parlo italiano *non parloh eetalyanoh*
Do you speak English?	Parla inglese? *parlah eengleseh*
What is the Italian for...?	Come si dice in italiano...? *komeh see deeche een eetalyanoh*
What's that?	Cos'è quello/a? *kozeh kwelloh/ah*
What's that called?	Come si chiama? *komeh see kyamah*
Can you tell me...	Mi può dire... *mee pwoh deereh*

TALKING ABOUT YOURSELF

I'm from...	Vengo da... *vengoh dah*
I'm...	Sono... *sonoh*
...English	...inglese *eengleseh*
...American	...americano/a *amereekanoh/ah*
...Canadian	...canadese *kanadezeh*
...Australian	...australiano/a *owstralyanoh/ah*
...single	...celibe/nubile *cheleebeh/noobeeleh*
...married	...sposato/a *sposatoh/ah*
...divorced	...divorziato/a *deevortsyatoh/ah*
I am...years old	Ho...anni *oh...annee*
I have...	Ho... *oh*
...a boyfriend	...un fidanzato *oon feedantsatoh*
...a girlfriend	...una fidanzata *oonah feedantsatah*

You may hear...

- **Da dove viene?**
  dah doveh vyeneh
  Where are you from?

- **È sposato/a?**
  eh sposatoh/ah
  Are you married?

- **Ha figli?**
  ah feelye
  Do you have children?

SOCIALIZING

Do you live here?	Vive qui? *veeveh kwee*
Where do you live?	Dove vive? *doveh veeveh*
I am here...	Sono qui... *sonoh kwee*
...on holiday	...in vacanza *een vakantsah*
...on business	...per lavoro *pehr lavoroh*
I'm a student	Sono uno/a studente/ studentessa *sonoh oonoh/ah stoodente/stoodentessah*
I work in...	Lavoro a... *lavoroh ah*
I am retired	Sono pensionato/a *sonoh penzyonatoh/ah*
Can I have...	Posso avere... *possoh avereh*
...your telephone number?	...il suo numero di telefono? *eel soowoh noomeroh dee telefonoh*
...your email address?	...il suo indirizzo e-mail? *eel soowoh eendeereedzo emayl*
It doesn't matter	Non importa *non eemportah*
Cheers	Cin cin *cheen cheen*
Do you mind if I smoke?	Le dispiace se fumo? *leh deespyache seh foomoh*
I don't drink/smoke	Non bevo/fumo *non bevoh/foomoh*
Are you alright?	Sta bene? *stah beneh*

LIKES AND DISLIKES

I like/love…	Mi piace/adoro… *mee pyacheh/adoroh*
I don't like…	Non mi piace… *non mee pyacheh*
I hate…	Detesto… *detestoh*
I quite/really like…	Mi piace abbastanza/molto… *mee pyacheh abbastantsa/moltoh*
Don't you like it?	Non le piace? *non leh pyacheh*
I would like…	Vorrei… *vorray*
My favourite is…	Il mio preferito è… *eel meeoh prefereetoh eh*
I prefer…	Preferisco… *prefereeskoh*
I think it's great	Penso che sia fantastico *penzoh keh sya fantasteeko*
It's delicious	È delizioso/a *eh deleetsyosoh/ah*
What would you like to do?	Cosa vorrebbe fare? *kozah vorrebbeh fareh*
I don't mind	Non mi dispiace *non mee deespyacheh*

You may hear…

- **Di cosa si occupa?**
  dee kozah see okoopah
  What do you do?

- **È in vacanza?**
  eh een vakantsah
  Are you on holiday?

- **Le piace…?**
  leh pyacheh
  Do you like…?

DAYS OF THE WEEK

What day is it today?	Che giorno è oggi? *keh jornoh eh ojee*
Sunday	domenica *domeneekah*
Monday	lunedì *loonedee*
Tuesday	martedì *martedee*
Wednesday	mercoledì *merkoledee*
Thursday	giovedì *jovedee*
Friday	venerdì *venerdee*
Saturday	sabato *sabatoh*
today	oggi *ojee*
tomorrow	domani *domanee*
yesterday	ieri *yeree*
in…days	tra…giorni *trah…jornee*

THE SEASONS

primavera
preemaverah
spring

estate
estateh
summer

MONTHS

January	gennaio *jenayo*
February	febbraio *febrayo*
March	marzo *martso*
April	aprile *apreeleh*
May	maggio *majjo*
June	giugno *joonyo*
July	luglio *loolyo*
August	agosto *agostoh*
September	settembre *setembreh*
October	ottobre *otobreh*
November	novembre *novembreh*
December	dicembre *deechembreh*

autunno
owtoonnoh
autumn

inverno
eenvernoh
winter

TELLING THE TIME

What time is it?	Che ore sono? *keh oreh sonoh*
It's nine o'clock	Sono le nove *sonoh leh noveh*
...in the morning	...del mattino *del matteenoh*
...in the afternoon	...del pomeriggio *del pomereedjoh*
...in the evening	...della sera *dellah serah*

l'una
loonah
one o'clock

l'una e dieci
loonah eh deeaychee
ten past one

l'una e un quarto
loonah eh oon kwartoh
quarter past one

l'una e venti
loonah eh ventee
twenty past one

l'una e mezza
loonah eh medza
half past one

due meno un quarto
dooeh menoh oon kwartoh
quarter to two

due meno dieci
dooeh menoh deeaychee
ten to two

le due
leh dooeh
two o'clock

It's midday/midnight	È mezzogiorno/mezzanotte *eh medzojornoh/ medzanotteh*
second	il secondo *eel sekondoh*
minute	il minuto *eel meenootoh*
hour	l'ora *lorah*
a quarter of an hour	un quarto d'ora *oon kwartoh dorah*
half an hour	mezz'ora *medzorah*
three-quarters of an hour	tre quarti d'ora *tray kwartee dorah*
late	tardi *tardee*
early/soon	presto/presto *prestoh*
What time does it start?	A che ora inizia? *ah keh orah eeneetsya*
What time does it finish?	A che ora finisce? *ah keh orah feeneesheh*
How long will it last?	Quanto tempo durerà? *kwantoh tempoh doorerah*

You may hear...

- **A presto.**
  ah prestoh
  See you later.

- **È in anticipo.**
  eh een anteecheepoh
  You're early.

- **È in ritardo.**
  eh een reetardoh
  You're late.

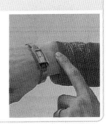

THE WEATHER

What's the forecast?	Quali sono le previsioni? *kwalee sonoh leh preveesyonee*
What's the weather like?	Che tempo fa? *ke tempoh fah*
It's...	È... *eh*
...good	...buono *bwonoh*
...bad	...cattivo *kateevoh*
...warm	...mite *meeteh*
...hot	...caldo *kaldoh*
...cold	...freddo *freddoh*

È soleggiato
eh solejatoh
It's sunny

È piovoso
eh pyovozoh
It's raining

È nuvoloso
eh noovolozoh
It's cloudy

È tempestoso
eh tempestozoh
It's stormy

What's the temperature?	Qual è la temperatura? *kwaleh lah temperatoorah*
It's...degrees	Ci sono...gradi *chee sonoh...gradee*
It's a beautiful day	È una bellissima giornata *eh oonah beleesseemah jornatah*
The weather's changing	Il tempo sta cambiando *eel tempoh stah kambyandoh*
Is it going to get colder/hotter?	Farà più freddo/caldo? *farah pew freddoh/kaldoh*
It's cooling down	La temperatura sta scendendo *lah temperatoorah stah shendendoh*

Nevica
neveeka
It's snowing

È ghiacciato
eh gyatchyatoh
It's icy

C'è nebbia
che nebbyah
It's misty

È ventoso
eh ventozoh
It's windy

GETTING AROUND

Italy has an excellent road and motorway system if you are travelling around the country by car, although you have to pay a toll (*un pedaggio*) to use the fast *autostrade* (motorways). Italian trains, linking the main towns and cities, are fast, punctual and surprisingly inexpensive. In large cities you can get around by taxi, bus or tram. In Milan there is also the underground (*metropolitana*).

ASKING WHERE THINGS ARE

Excuse me	Mi scusi *mee skoozee*
Where is…	Dov'è… *doveh*
…the town centre?	…il centro della città? *eel chentroh dellah cheetah*
…the railway station?	…la stazione ferroviaria? *lah statsyoneh ferovyarya*
…a cash machine?	…uno sportello bancomat? *oonoh sportelloh bankomat*
How do I get to…?	Come posso arrivare a…? *komeh possoh arreevareh ah*
I'm going to…	Sto andando a… *stoh andandoh ah*
I'm looking for…	Sto cercando… *stoh cherkandoh*
I'm lost	Mi sono perso/a *mee sonoh persoh/ah*
Is it near?	Si trova qui vicino? *see trovah kwee veecheenoh*
Is there a…nearby?	C'è un…qui vicino? *che oon…kwee veecheenoh*
Is it far?	È lontano? *eh lontanoh*
How far is…	Quanto dista… *kwantoh deestah*
…the town hall?	…il municipio? *eel mooneecheepyo*
…the market?	…il mercato? *eel merkatoh*
Can I walk there?	Posso arrivarci a piedi? *possoh arreevarchee ah pyedee*

CAR RENTAL

Where is the car rental desk?	Dov'è l'ufficio dell'autonoleggio? *doveh loofeechyo del owtonoledjoh*
I want to hire…	Vorrei noleggiare… *vorray noledjareh*
…a car	…un'automobile *oon owtomobeeleh*
…a bicycle	…una bicicletta *oonah beecheeklettah*

la berlina
lah berleenah
saloon car

il portellone posteriore
eel portelloneh posteryoreh
hatchback

il motociclo
eel motocheekloh
motorbike

lo scooter
loh scooter
scooter

la mountain bike
lah mountain bike
mountain bike

la bicicletta da strada
lah beecheeklettah dah stradah
road bike

for…days	per…giorni *pehr…jornee*
for a week	per una settimana *pehr oonah setteemanah*

for the weekend	per un fine settimana *pehr oon feeneh setteemanah*
I'd like...	Vorrei... *vorray*
...an automatic	...un'automobile con il cambio automatico *oon owtomobeeleh kon eel kambyo owtomateekoh*
...a manual	...un'automobile con il cambio manuale *oon owtomobeeleh kon eel kambyo manwaleh*
Here's my driving licence	Ecco la mia patente di guida *ekko lah mee-ah patenteh dee gweedah*
Can I hire a...	Posso noleggiare... *possoh noledjareh*
Do you have a...	Avete... *aveteh*

il seggiolino per bambini
eel sedjoleenoh pehr bambeenee
child seat

il lucchetto
eel lookettoh
lock

il casco
eel kaskoh
cycling helmet

DRIVING

Is this the road to...?	È questa la strada per...? *eh kwestah lah stradah pehr*
Where is the nearest garage?	Qual è l'officina più vicina? *kwaleh lofeecheenah pew veecheenah*
I'd like...	Vorrei... *vorray*
...some petrol	...del carburante *del karbooranteh*
...40 litres of unleaded	...quaranta litri di benzina senza piombo *kwarantah leetree dee bentseenah sentsah pyomboh*
...30 litres of diesel	...trenta litri di gasolio *trentah leetree dee gazolyo*
Fill it up, please	Il pieno, per favore *eel pyenoh, pehr favoreh*
Where do I pay?	Dove pago? *doveh pagoh?*
The pump number is...	La pompa numero... *lah pompah noomeroh...*
Can I pay by credit card?	Posso pagare con la carta di credito? *possoh pagareh kon lah kartah dee kredeetoh?*

la stazione di servizio
lah statsyoneh dee serveetsyo
petrol station

Can you check...	Può controllare...
	pwo kontrollareh
...the oil	...l'olio
	lolyo
...the tyre pressure	...la pressione dei pneumatici
	lah pressyoneh day pneuhmateechee

PARKING

Is there a car park nearby?	C'è un parcheggio nelle vicinanze?
	che oon parkedjo nelleh veecheenantse
Can I park here?	Posso parcheggiare qui?
	possoh parkedjare kwee
Is it free?	È gratuito?
	eh gratweetoh
How much does it cost?	Quanto costa?
	kwantoh kostah
How much is it...	Quanto costa...
	kwantoh kostah
...per hour?	...all'ora?
	alorah
...per day?	...al giorno?
	al jornoh
...overnight?	...fino al giorno dopo?
	feenoh al jornoh dopoh

il portapacchi
eel portapakee
roofrack

il seggiolino per bambini
eel sedjoleenoh pehr bambeenee
child seat

THE CAR

il bagagliaio
eel bagalyayo
boot

la marmitta
lah marmeetah
exhaust

la ruota
lah rwotah
wheel

lo sportello
loh sportelloh
door

INSIDE THE CAR

il poggiatesta
eel podjatestah
head rest

la maniglia
lah maneelya
handle

la chiusura
lah kewsoorah
door lock

il sedile posteriore
eel sedeeleh posteryoreh
back seat

la cintura di sicurezza
lah cheentoorah dee seekooredza
seat belt

il sedile anteriore
eel sedeeleh anteryoreh
front seat

il parabrezza
eel parabredza
windscreen

il cofano
eel kofanoh
bonnet

i fari
ee faree
headlights

il pneumatico
eel pneoomateekoh
tyre

il motore
eel motoreh
engine

il paraurti
eel parowrtee
bumper

THE CONTROLS

l'airbag
lairbag
airbag

le frecce lampeggianti
leh fretcheh lampedjantee
hazard lights

il cruscotto
eel krooskottoh
dashboard

lo sterzo
loh stertso
steering wheel

il tachimetro
eel takeemetroh
speedometer

il clacson
eel klakson
horn

la leva del cambio
lah levah del kambyo
gear stick

l'impianto stereo
leempyantoh stereo
car stereo

ROAD SIGNS

senso unico
senzoh ooneeko
one way

rotatoria
rotatorya
roundabout

dare la precedenza
dareh lah prechedentsa
give way

divieto di sosta
deevyetoh dee sostah
no stopping

divieto di accesso
deevyetoh dee atchessoh
no entry

sosta vietata
sostah vyetatah
no parking

limite di velocità
leemeeteh dee velocheetah
speed limit

pericolo
pereekoloh
hazard

l'autostrada
lowtostradah
motorway

la bretella
lah bretellah
sliproad

ON THE ROAD

il parchimetro
eel parkeemetroh
parking meter

il semaforo
eel semaforoh
traffic light

il vigile
eel veejeeleh
traffic policeman

la cartina
lah karteenah
map

l'attraversamento pedonale
latraversamentoh pedonaleh
pedestrian crossing

il telefono di emergenza
eel telefonoh dee emerjentsa
emergency phone

l'ingorgo stradale
leengorgoh stradahleh
traffic jam

il parcheggio per disabili
eel parkedjoh pehr deezabeelee
disabled parking

AT THE STATION

Where can I buy a ticket?	Dove posso acquistare un biglietto? *doveh possoh akweestareh oon beelyettoh*
Is there an automatic ticket machine?	C'è una biglietteria automatica? *che oonah beelyettereeya owtomateekah*

la biglietteria automatica
lah beelyetterya owtomateekah
automatic ticket machine

il biglietto
eel beelyettoh
ticket

Two tickets to…	Due biglietti per… *dooeh beelyettee pehr*
I'd like…	Vorrei… *vorray*
…a single ticket to…	…un biglietto di sola andata per… *oon beelyettoh dee solah andatah pehr*
…a return ticket to…	…un biglietto di andata e ritorno per… *oon beelyettoh dee andatah eh reetornoh pehr*
…a first class ticket	…un biglietto di prima classe *oon beelyettoh dee preemah klasseh*
…a standard class ticket	…un biglietto di classe economica *oon beelyettoh dee klasseh ekonomeekah*

I'd like to...	Vorrei... *vorray*
...reserve a seat	...prenotare un posto *prenotareh oon postoh*
...on the Eurostar to...	...sull'Eurostar per... *soolehoorostar pehr*
...book a couchette	...prenotare una cuccetta *prenotareh oonah koochettah*
Is there a reduction...?	C'è una riduzione... *che oonah reedootsyoneh*
...for children?	...per i bambini? *pehr ee bambeenee*
...for students?	...per gli studenti? *pehr lyee stoodentee*
...for senior citizens?	...per gli anziani? *pehr lyee antsyaneh*
Is there a restaurant car?	C'è una carrozza ristorante? *che oonah karrodza reestoranteh*
Is it a fast/slow train?	È un treno rapido/locale? *eh oon trenoh rapeedoh/ lokaleh*
Do I stamp the ticket before boarding?	Devo vidimare il biglietto prima di salire in carrozza? *devoh veedeemareh eel beelyettoh preemah dee saleereh een karrodza*

You may hear...

- Il treno parte dal binario...
  eel trenoh parteh dal beenaryo
  The train leaves from platform...

- Deve cambiare treno.
  deveh kambyareh trenoh
  You must change trains.

TRAVELLING BY TRAIN

Do you have a timetable?	Ha un orario? *ah oon oraryo*
What time is...	A che ora è... *ah ke orah eh*
...the next train to...?	...il prossimo treno per...? *eel prosseemoh trenoh pehr*
...the last train to...?	...l'ultimo treno per...? *loolteemoh trenoh pehr*
Which platform does it leave from?	Da quale binario parte? *dah kwaleh beenaryo parteh*
What time does it arrive in...?	A che ora arriva a...? *a ke orah arreevah ah*
How long does it take?	Quanto tempo ci impiega? *kwantoh tempoh chee eempyegah*
Is this the train for...?	È questo il treno per...? *eh kwestoh eel trenoh pehr*
Is this the right platform for...?	È questo il binario giusto per...? *eh kwestoh eel beenaryo jewstoh pehr*
Where is platform three?	Dov'è il binario tre? *doveh eel beenaryo treh*
Does this train stop at...?	Questo treno ferma a...? *kwestoh trenoh fermah ah*

You may hear...

- Deve vidimare il biglietto.
  deveh veedeemareh eel beelyettoh
  You must validate your ticket.

- Usi la macchinetta gialla.
  oozee lah makeenettah jallah
  Use the yellow machine.

Where do I change for…?	Dove devo cambiare per…? *doveh devoh kambyareh pehr*
Is this seat free?	È libero questo posto? *eh leeberoh kwestoh postoh*
I've reserved this seat	Ho prenotato questo posto *oh prenotatoh kwestoh postoh*
Do I get off here?	Devo scendere qui? *devoh shendereh kwee*
Where is the underground station?	Dov'è la stazione della metropolitana? *doveh lah statsyoneh dellah metropoleetanah*
Which line goes to…?	Quale linea arriva a…? *kwaleh leeneah arrivah ah*
How many stops is it?	Quante fermate sono? *kwanteh fermateh sonoh*

l'atrio
latryo
concourse

il treno
eel trenoh
train

la carrozza ristorante
lah karrodzah reestoranteh
dining car

la cuccetta
lah kootchettah
couchette

BUSES

When is the next bus to…?	Quando parte il prossimo autobus per…? *kwandoh parteh eel prosseemoh owtoboos pehr*
What is the fare to…?	Quanto costa un biglietto per…? *kwantoh kostah oon beelyettoh pehr*
Where is the bus stop?	Dov'è la fermata dell'autobus? *doveh lah fermatah del owtoboos*
Is this the bus stop for…	È questa la fermata dell'autobus per…? *eh kwestah lah fermatah del owtoboos pehr*
Where can I buy a ticket?	Dove posso acquistare un biglietto? *doveh possoh akweestareh oon beelyettoh*
Can I pay on the bus?	Posso pagare sull'autobus? *possoh pagareh soolowtoboos*
Which buses go to the city centre?	Quali autobus raggiungono il centro? *kwalee owtoboos radjewngonoh eel chentroh*
Will you tell me when to get off?	Mi può dire quando devo scendere? *mee pwo deereh kwandoh devoh shendereh*

l'autobus
lowtoboos
bus

la stazione degli autobus
lah statsyoneh delyee owtoboos
bus station

TAXIS

Can I order a taxi?	Dove posso richiedere un taxi? *doveh possoh reekyedereh oon taxi*
I want a taxi to…	Desidero un taxi per… *deseederoh oon taxi pehr*
Can you take me to…	Mi può portare a/in… *mee pwo portareh ah/een*
Is it far?	È lontano? *eh lontanoh*
How much will it cost?	Quanto costa? *kwantoh kostah*
Can you drop me here?	Mi può far scendere qui? *mee pwo far shendereh kwee*
What do I owe you?	Quanto le devo? *kwantoh leh devoh*
I don't have any change	Non ho spiccioli *non oh speetchyolee*
Keep the change	Tenga il resto *tengah eel restoh*
Please can I have a receipt	Potrei avere la ricevuta, per favore *potray avereh lah reechevootah pehr favoreh*
Please wait for me	Mi aspetti, per favore *mee aspeteeh pehr favoreh*

il taxi
eel taxee
taxi

BOATS

Are there any boat trips?	Ci sono navi in partenza? *chee sonoh navee een partentsa*
Where does the boat leave from?	Dove parte la nave? *doveh parteh lah naveh*
When is…	Quando parte… *kwandoh parteh*
…the next boat to…?	…la prossima nave per…? *lah prosseemah naveh pehr*
…the first boat?	…la prima nave? *lah preemah naveh*
…the last boat?	…l'ultima nave? *loolteemah naveh*
I'd like two tickets for…	Vorrei due biglietti per… *vorray dooeh beelyettee pehr*
…the cruise	…la crociera *lah crotchyerah*

il traghetto
eel tragettoh
ferry

l'aliscafo
laleeskafoh
hydrofoil

lo yacht
loh yacht
yacht

l'hovercraft
lovercraft
hovercraft

...the river trip	...la gita sul fiume *lah jeetah sool fewmeh*
How much is it for...	Quanto costa per... *kwantoh kostah pehr*
...a car and two people?	...un'automobile e due persone? *oon owtomobeeleh eh dooeh personeh*
...a family?	...una famiglia? *oona fameelyah*
...a cabin	...una cabina *oonah kabeenah*
Can I buy a ticket on board?	Posso acquistare il biglietto a bordo? *possoh akweestareh eel beelyettoh ah bordoh*
Is there wheelchair access?	C'è un accesso per disabili? *che oon atchessoh pehr deezabeelee*

il giubbotto di salvataggio
eel jewbottoh dee salvatadjoh
life jacket

il salvagente
eel salvajenteh
lifebuoy

il catamarano
eel katamaranoh
catamaran

Il motoscafo
eel motoscarfoh
motorboat

AIR TRAVEL

Which terminal do I need?	A quale terminal devo andare? *ah kwaleh terminahl devoh andareh*
Where do I check in?	Dove posso effettuare il check-in? *doveh possoh effetwareh eel check-in*
Where is...	Dove si trovano... *doveh see trovanoh*
...the arrivals hall?	...gli arrivi? *lyee arreevee*
...the departures hall?	...le partenze? *leh partentse*
...the boarding gate?	...le uscite d'imbarco? *leh oosheeteh deembarkoh*
I'm travelling...	Viaggio... *vyajoh*
...economy	...in classe economica *een klasseh ekonomeeka*

la sacca da viaggio
lah sakah dah vyajo
holdall

il pasto a bordo
eel pastoh ah bordoh
flight meal

il passaporto
eel passaportoh
passport

la carta d'imbarco
lah kartah deembarko
boarding pass

I'm checking in one suitcase	Desidero imbarcare un bagaglio *deseederoh eembarkareh oon bagalyo*
I packed it myself	Ho preparato io il bagaglio *oh preparatoh eeoh eel bagalyo*
I have one piece of hand luggage	Ho un unico bagaglio a mano *oh oon ooneeko bagalyo ah manoh*
How much is excess baggage?	A quanto ammonta il peso in eccesso? *ah kwantoh amontah eel pezoh een etchessoh*
Will a meal be served?	Sarà servito un pasto? *sarah serveetoh oon pastoh*
I'd like...	Vorrei... *vorray*
...a window seat	...un posto vicino al finestrino *oon postoh veecheenoh al feenestreenoh*
...an aisle seat	...un posto vicino al corridoio *oon postoh veecheenoh al koreedoyo*

You may hear...

- Il suo passaporto/biglietto, per favore.
  eel soowo passaportoh/ beelyettoh pehr favoreh
  Your passport/ticket, please.

- È sua questa borsa?
  eh soowa kwestah borsah
  Is this your bag?

AT THE AIRPORT

Here's my...	Ecco... *ekko*
...boarding pass	...la mia carta d'imbarco *la meeah karta deembarkoh*
...passport	...il mio passaporto *eel meeoh passaportoh*
Can I change some money?	Potrei cambiare del denaro? *potray kambyareh dehl denaroh?*

traveller's cheque
traveller's cheque
traveller's cheque

il controllo passaporti
eel kontrolloh passaportee
passport control

What is the exchange rate?	Qual è il tasso di cambio? *kwaleh eel tassoh dee kambyo*
Is the flight delayed?	Il volo è in ritardo? *eel voloh eh een reetardoh*
How late is it?	Quanto porta di ritardo? *kwantoh portah dee reetardoh*
Which gate does flight... leave from?	Qual è l'uscita del volo...? *kwaleh loosheetah del voloh*
What time do I board?	A che ora ci imbarchiamo? *ah keh orah chee eembarkyamoh*
When does the gate close?	Quando chiude l'uscita d'imbarco? *kwandoh kewdeh loosheetah deembarkoh*

Where are the trolleys?	Dove sono i carrelli? *doveh sonoh ee karrelee*
Here is the reclaim tag	Ecco la ricevuta dei bagagli *ekko lah reechevootah day bagalye*
I can't find my baggage	Non trovo i miei bagagli *non trovoh ee myeh-ee bagalye*

il negozio duty-free
eel negotsyo dootee free
duty-free shop

il pilota
eel peelotah
pilot

l'assistente di volo
lasseestenteh dee voloh
air stewardess

l'aeroplano
lahehroplahnoh
aeroplane

banco del check-in
banko del chek een
check-in desk

il ritiro bagagli
eel reeteeroh bagalye
baggage reclaim

EATING OUT

It is not difficult to eat well and inexpensively in Italy. You can choose from cafés and bars, which serve a variety of drinks, snacks and light meals, *osterie* and *trattorie* (small family-run restaurants which serve local and traditional dishes) and *pizzerie* (for pizzas and pasta). If you want a gastronomic meal in more formal surroundings, you can eat at more expensive *ristorante* but you may have to book in advance at the popular ones.

MAKING A RESERVATION

I'd like to book a table…	Vorrei prenotare un tavolo… *voray prenotareh oon tavoloh*
…for lunch/dinner	…per pranzo/cena *pehr prandzo/ chenah*
…for four people	…per quattro persone *pehr kwatroh perzoneh*
…for this evening	…per questa sera *pehr kwestah serah*
…for tomorrow at one	…per l'una di domani *pehr loonah dee domanee*
…for today	…per oggi *pehr ojee*
Do you have a table earlier/later?	Ha un tavolo prima/più tardi? *ah oon tavoloh preemah/ pew tardee*
My name is…	Il cognome è… *eel konyomeh eh*
My telephone number is…	Il mio numero di telefono è… *eel meeoh noomeroh dee telefonoh eh*
Do you take credit cards?	Accettate carte di credito? *atchettateh karteh dee kredeetoh*
I have a reservation	Ho una prenotazione *oh oonah prenotatsyoneh*
in the name of…	a nome di… *ah nomeh dee*
We haven't booked	Non abbiamo prenotato *non abyamoh prenotatoh*
Can we sit here?	Possiamo sederci qui? *possyamoh sederchee kwee*
We'd like to eat outside	Vorremmo mangiare fuori *vorremoh manjareh fworee*

ORDERING A MEAL

Can we see the menu?	Possiamo vedere il menù? *possyamoh vedereh eel menoo*
...the wine list?	...la carta dei vini? *lah kartah day veenee*
Do you have...	Ha... *ah*
...a set menu?	...un menù fisso? *oon menoo feesoh*
...a fixed-price menu?	...un menù a prezzo fisso? *oon menoo ah predzo feesoh*
...a children's menu?	...un menù per bambini? *oon menoo pehr bambeenee*
...an à la carte menu	...un menù alla carta? *oon menoo allah kartah*
What are today's specials?	Qual è la specialità del giorno? *kwaleh lah spechyaleetah del jornoh*
What is this?	Cos'è questo/a? *kozeh kwestoh/ah*

You may hear...

- **Ha prenotato?**
  ah prenotatoh
  Do you have a reservation?

- **A nome di?**
  ah nomeh dee
  In what name?

- **Si sieda per favore**
  see syedah pehr favoreh
  Please be seated

- **Vuole ordinare?**
  wwoleh ordeenareh
  Are you ready to order?

Are there any vegetarian dishes?	Avete dei piatti vegetariani? *aveteh day pyateh vejetaryanee*
I can't eat...	Non posso mangiare... *non possoh manjareh*
...dairy foods	...i latticini *ee latteecheenee*
...nuts	...la frutta secca *lah frootah sekah*
...wheat	...il frumento *eel froomentoh*
To drink, I'll have...	Da bere, vorrei... *dah bereh vorray*
Can we have...	Possiamo avere... *possyamoh avereh*
...some water	...dell'acqua? *delakwa*
...some bread?	...del pane? *del paneh*
...the dessert menu?	...il menù dei dolci? *eel menoo day dolchee*

Reading the menu

• Gli antipasti *lyee anteepastee*	Starters
• I primi *ee preemee*	First courses
• I secondi *ee sekondee*	Main courses
• I contorni *ee kontornee*	Vegetables
• I formaggi *ee formadjee*	Cheeses
• I dolci *ee dolchee*	Desserts

COMPLAINING

I didn't order this	Non ho ordinato questo/a *non oh ordeenatoh kwestoh/ah*
When is our food coming?	Quando arriva il cibo? *kwandoh arreevah eel cheeboh*
We can't wait any longer	Non possiamo aspettare oltre *non possyamoh aspettareh oltreh*

PAYING

The bill, please	Il conto, per favore *eel kontoh pehr favoreh*
Can we pay separately?	Possiamo pagare separatamente? *possyamoh pagareh separatamenteh*
Can I have...	Posso avere... *possoh avereh*
...a receipt?	...la ricevuta? *lah reechevootah*
...an itemized bill?	...una ricevuta dettagliata? *oonah reechevootah detalyatah*
Is service included?	Il servizio è incluso? *eel serveetsyo eh eenkloozoh*

You may hear...

- **Non accettiamo carte di credito.**
  non atchetyamoh karteh dee kredeetoh
  We don't take credit cards.

- **Digiti il PIN.**
  deejeetee eel peen
  Please enter your PIN.

CROCKERY AND CUTLERY

il piattino
eel pyateenoh
side plate

la scodella
lah skodellah
bowl

il pepe
eel pepeh
pepper

il sale
eel saleh
salt

la tazza e il piattino
lah tadza eh eel pyateenoh

il cucchiaino
eel kookyaeenoh
teaspoon

il bicchiere
eel beekyereh
glass

il cucchiaio
eel kookyayo
dessertspoon

il coltello
eel koltelloh
knife

il tovagliolo
eel tovalyoloh
napkin

la forchetta
lah forkettah
fork

il piatto piano
eel pyato pyanoh
dinner plate

AT THE CAFÉ OR BAR

The menu, please	Il menù, per favore *eel menooh pehr favoreh*
Do you have...?	Ha...? *ah*
What fruit juices/herb teas do you have?	Quali succhi di frutta/tisane ha? *kwalee sookee dee frootah/ teezaneh ah*
I'd like...	Vorrei... *vorray*

un caffellatte
oon kaffelatteh
white coffee

un caffè
oon kaffeh
black coffee

un espresso
oon espressoh
espresso

un cappuccino
oon kapootcheenoh
cappuccino

You may hear...

- **Cosa desidera?**
  kozah deseederah
  What would you like?

- **Altro?**
  altroh
  Anything else?

- **Prego.**
  pregoh
  You're welcome.

un tè al latte
oon teh al latteh
tea with milk

un tè al limone
oon teh al leemoneh
tea with lemon

un tè alla menta
oon teh allah mentah
mint tea

un tè verde
oon teh verdeh
green tea

una camomilla
oonah kamomeelah
camomile tea

una cioccolata calda
oonah chokolatah kaldah
hot chocolate

A bottle of…	Una bottiglia di… *oonah botteelya dee*
A glass of…	Un bicchiere di… *oon beekyereh dee*
A cup of…	Una tazza di… *oonah tadza dee*
With lemon/milk	con limone/latte *kon leemoneh/latteh*
Another…please	Un altro/a…per favore *oon altroh/ah…pehr favoreh*
The same again, please	Me ne porta ancora, per favore *meh neh portah ankorah pehr favoreh*

CAFÉ AND BAR DRINKS

un caffè shakerato
oon kaffeh shakeratoh
iced coffee

una spremuta d'arancia
oonah spremootah daranchya
fresh orange juice

un succo di mela
oon sookoh dee melah
apple juice

un succo di ananas
oon sookoh dee ananas
pineapple juice

un succo di pomodoro
oon sookoh dee pomodoroh
tomato juice

un succo d'uva
oon sookoh doovah
grape juice

una limonata
oonah leemonatah
lemonade

un crodino
oon krodeenoh
Crodino

una coca cola
oonah kokakolah
cola

un prosecco
oon prosekoh
sparkling wine

acqua minerale
akwa meeneraleh
mineral water

una grappa
oonah grappah
Grappa

una birra
oonah beerrah
beer

un campari
oon kamparee
Campari

un vino rosso
oon veenoh rossoh
red wine

un vino bianco
oon veenoh byankoh
white wine

You may hear...

- **In bottiglia o alla spina?**
  een botteelya oh allah speenah
  Bottled or draught?

- **Liscia o gassata?**
  leesha oh gassatah
  Still or sparkling?

- **Con ghiaccio?**
  kon gyachyo
  With ice?

BAR SNACKS

un tramezzino
oon tramedzeenoh
sandwich

un panino
oon paneenoh
panino

le olive
leh oliveh
olives

le noccioline
leh notcholeeneh
nuts

il condimento
eel kondimentoh
dressing

l'insalata
leensalatah
salad

i biscotti
ee beeskottee
biscuits

la bruschetta
lah brooskettah
bruschetta

il gelato
eel jelatoh
ice cream

i maritozzi
ee mareetodzee
cream buns

FAST FOOD

Can I have…

Posso avere…
possoh avereh

…to eat in/take away

…da mangiare qui/da
portare via
*dah manjareh kwee/dah
portareh vee-ah*

un hamburger
oon amboorger
hamburger

un hamburger di pollo
oon amboorger dee polloh
chicken burger

una piadina arrotolata
oonah pyadeenah arotolatah
wrap

un hot dog
oon otdog
hot dog

un kebab
oon kebab
kebab

le patatine
leh patateeneh
French fries

il pollo fritto
eel polloh freetoh
fried chicken

la pizza
lah peedza
pizza

BREAKFAST

Can I have...	Posso avere... *possoh avereh*
...some milk	...del latte? *del latteh*
...some sugar	dello zucchero? *delloh tsookeroh*
...some artificial sweetener	...del dolcificante? *del dolcheefeekanteh*
...some butter	...del burro? *del booroh*
...some jam?	...della marmellata? *dellah marmellatah*
...some salt/pepper?	...del sale/del pepe? *del saleh/del pehpeh*

un caffè
oon kaffeh
coffee

un tè
oon teh
tea

una cioccolata calda
oonah chokolatah kaldah
hot chocolate

una spremuta d'arancia
oonah spremootah daranchya
orange juice

un succo di mela
oon sookoh dee melah
apple juice

il pane
eel paneh
bread

un cornetto
oon kornettoh
croissant

un cornetto al cioccolato
oon kornettoh al chokolatoh
chocolate croissant

la marmellata
lah marmellatah
marmalade

un panino
oon paneenoh
bread roll

le uova strapazzate
leh wovah strapadzateh
scrambled eggs

il miele
eel myeleh
honey

l'uovo in camicia
lwovoh een kameecha
poached egg

l'uovo sodo
lwovoh sodoh
boiled egg

la frutta fresca
lah frootah freskah
fresh fruit

lo yoghurt alla frutta
loh yogoort allah frootah
fruit yoghurt

FIRST COURSES

la minestra
lah meenestrah
soup

il brodo
eel brodoh
broth

la zuppa di pesce
lah tsoopah dee pesheh
fish soup

il minestrone
eel meenestroneh
minestrone

gli gnocchi
lyee nyokee
gnocchi

la frittata
lah freetatah
omelette

la bresaola
lah bresaolah
bresaola

il risotto
eel reezottoh
risotto

il prosciutto crudo
eel proshewtoh kroodoh
cured ham

i gamberi alla griglia
ee gamberee allah greelya
grilled prawns

l'antipasto di mare
lanteepastoh dee mareh
seafood antipasto

le sarde al saor
leh sardeh al saor
Venetian-style sardines

l'antipasto misto
lanteepastoh meestoh
mixed antipasto

l'antipasto freddo
lanteepastoh freddoh
antipasto of cold meats

gli spaghetti alla vongole
lyee spagetee alla vongoleh
spaghetti with clams

gli spaghetti alla carbonara
lyee spagetee alla karbonara
spaghetti carbonara

gli spaghetti alla bolognese
lyee spagetee alla bolonyeseh
spaghetti bolognese

la bagna cauda
lah banya cowdah
hot anchovy dip

i cannelloni
ee kannellonee
cannelloni

i tortelloni
ee tortellonee
tortelloni

MAIN COURSES

I would like...	Vorrei... *vorray*
...the chicken	...il pollo *eel polloh*
...the duck	...l'anatra *lanatrah*
...the lamb	...l'agnello *lanyelloh*
...the pork	...il maiale *eel mayaleh*
...the beef	...il manzo *eel mandzo*
...the steak	...la bistecca *lah beestekkah*
...the veal	...il vitello *eel veeteloh*
...the liver	...il fegato *eel fegatoh*
roast	arrosto *arrostoh*
baked	al forno *al fornoh*
grilled	alla griglia *allah greelya*
on skewers	allo spiedo *alloh spyedoh*

You may see...

i frutti di mare
ee frootee dee mareh
seafood

il pesce
eel pesheh
fish

You may hear...

- **Come desidera la bistecca?**
  komeh deseederah lah beestekkah
  How do you like your steak?

- **Al sangue, a cottura media o ben cotta?**
  al sangweh, ah kottoorah medya oh ben kottah
  Rare, medium rare or well done?

barbecued	al barbecue *al barbekew*
poached	in camicia *een kameechya*
boiled	lesso/sodo *lessoh/sodoh*
fried	fritto *freetoh*
pan-fried/sautéed	in padella/saltato *een padellah/saltatoh*
stuffed	farcito *farcheetoh*
stewed	stufato *stoofatoh*
...with Parmesan cheese	...con il parmigiano *kon eel parmeejanoh*

il pollame
eel pollameh
poultry

la carne
lah karneh
meat

SALADS AND SIDE DISHES

l'insalata verde
leensalatah verdeh
green salad

l'insalata mista
leensalatah meestah
mixed salad

il radicchio alla griglia
eel radeekkyo allah greelya
grilled radicchio

le verdure al vapore
leh verdooreh al vaporeh
steamed vegetables

il riso
eel reezoh
rice

la pasta
lah pastah
pasta

le patatine fritte
leh patateeneh freeteh
chips

gli spinaci
lyee speenachee
spinach

gli asparagi
lyee asparajee
asparagus

la polenta
lah polentah
polenta

DESSERTS

la mousse di cioccolato
lah moos dee chokolatoh
chocolate mousse

la cassata
lah kassatah
cassata

la crostata di nocciole
lah krostatah dee nochyoleh
hazelnut tart

la crostata di ricotta
lah krostatah dee reekottah
ricotta tart

il sorbetto
eel sorbettoh
sorbet

il gelato
eel jelatoh
ice cream

il tiramisù
eel teerameesoo
tiramisù

la torta
lah tortah
cake

la crostata di frutta
lah krostatah dee frootah
fruit tart

lo zabaglione
loh tsabalyoneh
zabaglione

PLACES TO STAY

Italy has a wide range of places to stay, depending
on your personal preference and budget. These
range from elegant hotels in former *palazzi* to
smaller *alberghi*, *locande* (one-star hotels) and
family-run *pensioni*. If you want a self-catering
option, however, you can choose to rent a seaside
apartment or a country villa, or find a campsite
to park your caravan or put up your tent.

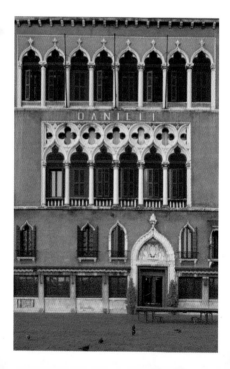

MAKING A RESERVATION

I'd like...	Vorrei... *vorray*
...to make a reservation	...fare una prenotazione *fareh oonah prenotatsyoneh*
...a double room	...una camera doppia *oonah kamerah doppya*
...a twin-bedded room	...una camera a due letti *oonah kamerah ah dooeh lettee*
...a single room	...una camera singola *oonah kamerah seengolah*
...a family room	...una camera familiare *oonah kamerah fameelyareh*
...a disabled person's room	...una camera per disabili *oonah kamerah pehr deezabeelee*
...with a bath/shower	...con bagno/doccia *kon banyo/dotchya*
...with a sea view	...con vista sul mare *kon veestah sool mareh*
...with a balcony	...con balcone *kon balkoneh*
...for two nights	...per due notti *pehr dooeh nottee*
...for a week	...per una settimana *pehr oonah setteemanah*
Is breakfast included?	La colazione è inclusa? *lah kolatsyoneh eh eenkloosah*
How much is it...	Quanto costa... *kwantoh kostah*
...per night?	...a notte? *ah notteh*
...per week?	...alla settimana? *allah setteemanah*

CHECKING IN

I have a reservation in the name of…	Ho una prenotazione a nome di… *oh oonah prenotatsyoneh ah nomeh dee*

Do you have…	Ha… *ah*

un facchino
oon fakeenoh
a porter

gli ascensori
lyee ashenzoree
lifts

il servizio in camera
eel serveetsyo een kamerah
room service

il mini bar
eel meenee bar
mini bar

I'd like…	Vorrei… *vorray*
…the keys for room…	…le chiavi della camera… *leh kyaveh dellah kamerah*
…a wake-up call at…	…la sveglia alle… *lah svelya alleh*
What time is…	A che ora servite… *ah ke orah serveeteh*
…breakfast?	…la colazione? *lah kolatsyoneh*
…dinner?	…la cena? *lah chenah*

IN YOUR ROOM

Do you have…	Ha… *ah*
another…	un altro/a… *oon altroh/ah*
some more…	altri/e… *altree/eh*

i cuscini
ee koosheenee
pillows

le coperte
leh koperteh
blankets

una lampadina
oonah lampadeenah
a light bulb

un adattatore
oon adatatoreh
an adapter

I've lost my key

Ho perso la mia chiave
oh persoh lah meeah kiaveh

You may hear...

- Il suo numero di camera è…
  eel soo-oh noomeroh dee kamerah eh
  Your room number is…

- Ecco la sua chiave.
  ekko lah sooah kiaveh
  Here is your key.

IN THE HOTEL

The room is…	La camera è… *lah kamerah e*
…too hot	…troppo calda *troppoh kaldah*
…too cold	…troppo fredda *troppoh freddah*
…too small	…troppo piccola *troppoh peekolah*

il termostato
eel termostatoh
thermostat

il radiatore
eel radyatoreh
radiator

la camera singola
lah kamerah seengolah
single room

la camera doppia
lah kamerah doppya
double room

il numero della camera
eel noomeroh dellah kamerah
room number

il bollitore
eel bolleetoreh
kettle

The window won't open	La finestra non si apre *lah feenestrah non see apreh*
The TV doesn't work	Il televisore non funziona *eel televeezoreh non funtsyonah*

l'appendiabiti
lappendeeabeetee
coat hanger

il televisore
eel televeezoreh
television

la veneziana
lah venetsyanah
venetian blind

il telecomando
eel telekomandoh
remote control

CHECKING OUT

When do I have to vacate the room?	Quando devo lasciare la stanza? *kwandoh devoh lasheeareh lah standza*
Is there a porter to carry my bags?	C'è un facchino per portare le mie valigie? *che oon fakkeenoh pehr portareh leh meeye valeejeh*
Can I have the bill, please?	Posso avere il conto? *possoh avereh eel kontoh*
Can I pay…	Posso pagare… *possoh pagareh*
…by credit card?	…con la carta di credito? *kon lah kartah dee kredeetoh*
…cash?	…in contanti? *een kontantee*
I'd like a receipt	Vorrei la ricevuta *vorray lah reechevootah*

IN THE BATHROOM

la vasca da bagno
lah vaska dah banyo
bathtub

il bidet
eel beedeh
bidet

il sapone
eel saponeh
soap

gli asciugamani
lyee ashewgamanee
towels

l'accappatoio
lakappatoyo
bathrobe

il bagnoschiuma
eel banyoskewmah
bubblebath

il docciaschiuma
eel dotchyaskwemah
shower gel

il deodorante
eel dehodoranteh
deodorant

la crema per il corpo
lah kremah pehr eel korpoh
body lotion

il dentifricio
eel denteefreechyo
toothpaste

lo spazzolino da denti
loh spatsoleenoh dah dentee
toothbrush

il colluttorio
eel kolootoryo
mouthwash

il rasoio elettrico
eel rasoyo eletreeko
electric razor

la schiuma da barba
lah skewmah dah barbah
shaving foam

il rasoio
eel rasoyo
razor

l'asciugacapelli
lashewgakapellee
hairdryer

lo shampoo
loh shampoh
shampoo

il balsamo
eel balsamoh
conditioner

il tagliaunghie
eel talyaoongye
nail clippers

le forbici per unghie
leh forbeechee pehr oongye
nail scissors

SELF-CATERING

Can we have…	Possiamo avere… *possyamoh avereh*
…the key, please?	…la chiave, per favore? *lah kiaveh pehr favoreh*
…an extra bed?	…un letto extra? *oon lettoh extrah*
…a child's bed?	…un lettino? *oon letteenoh*

il seggiolone
eel sedjoloneh
high chair

il lettino
eel leteenoh
cot

…more cutlery, crockery	…più posate, stoviglie *pew posateh stoveelye*
Where is…	Dov'è… *doveh*
…the fusebox?	…la scatola dei fusibili? *lah skatolah day fooseebeelee*
…the stopcock?	…il rubinetto d'arresto? *eel roobeenettoh darrestoh*
…the nearest shop?	…il negozio più vicino? *eel negotsyo pew veecheenoh*
Do you do babysitting?	Offrite un servizio di babysitting? *offreeteh oon serveetsyo dee babyseetteeng*
How does the heating work?	Come funziona il riscaldamento? *komeh foontsyonah eel reeskaldamentoh*

Is there...	C'è... *che*
...air conditioning?	...l'aria condizionata? *larya kondeetsyonatah*
...central heating?	...il riscaldamento centralizzato? *eel reeskaldamentoh chentraleedzatoh*

il ventilatore
eel venteelatoreh
fan

il termoconvettore
eel termokonverteetoreh
convector heater

When does the cleaner come?	Quando passa l'addetto alle pulizie? *kwandoh passah ladettoh alleh pooleetsye*
Where do I put the rubbish?	Dove posso buttare l'immondizia? *doveh possoh bootareh leemondeetsyah*
Do you take pets?	Accettate animali domestici? *atchettateh aneemalee domesteechee*

il cane
eel kaneh
dog

IN THE VILLA

Is there an inventory?	C'è un inventario? *che oon eenventaryo*
Where is this item?	Dove si trova questo articolo? *doveh see trovah kwestoh arteekoloh*
I need...	Ho bisogno di... *oh beezonyo dee*
...an extension lead	...una prolunga *oonah proloongah*
...a torch	...una torcia *oonah torchya*
...matches	...dei fiammiferi *day fyameeferee*

il forno a microonde
eel fornoh ah meekrohondeh
microwave

il ferro da stiro
eel ferroh dah steeroh
iron

l'asse da stiro
lasseh dah steeroh
ironing board

il mocio e il secchio
eel mochyo eh eel sekkyo
mop and bucket

la paletta e la scopetta
lah palettah eh lah skopettah
dust pan and brush

il detersivo
eel deterseevoh
detergent

PROBLEM SOLVING

The shower doesn't work	La doccia non funziona *lah dotchya non foontsyonah*
The toilet is leaking	Il water perde acqua *eel vater perdeh akwa*
Can you mend it today?	Può aggiustarlo oggi? *pwo adjewstarloh ojee*
There's no...	Non c'è... *non che*
...electricity/gas	...elettricità/gas *eletreecheetah/gas*
...water	...acqua *akwa*

la lavatrice
lah lavatreeche
washing machine

il frigorifero
eel freegoreeferoh
fridge

la pattumiera
lah patoomyerah
rubbish bin

il lucchetto e la chiave
eel lookettoh eh lah kiaveh
lock and key

il rivelatore di fumo
eel reevelatoreh dee foomoh
smoke alarm

l'estintore
lesteentoreh
fire extinguisher

KITCHEN EQUIPMENT

l'apriscatole
lapreeskatoleh
can opener

l'apribottiglie
lapreeboteelyeh
bottle opener

il cavatappi
eel kavatappee
corkscrew

il tagliere
eel talyehreh
chopping board

il coltello da cucina
eel koltelloh dah koocheenah
kitchen knife

lo sbucciatore
loh sboochyatoreh
peeler

la frusta
lah froostah
whisk

il cucchiaio di legno
eel kookyayo dee lenyo
wooden spoon

la spatola
lah spatolah
spatula

la grattuggia
lah grattoojah
grater

il colapasta
eel kolapastah
colander

la padella
lah padellah
frying pan

la pentola
la pentolah
saucepan

la griglia
lah greelya
grill pan

la casseruola
lah kasserwolah
casserole dish

l'insalatiera
leensalatyerah
mixing bowl

il frullatore
eel froolatoreh
blender

la teglia da forno
lah telya dah fornoh
baking tray

i guanti da forno
ee gwanteh dah fornoh
oven gloves

il grembiule
eel grembewleh
apron

CAMPING

Where is the nearest…	Dov'è il più vicino… *doveh eel pew veecheenoh*
…campsite?	…campeggio? *kampedjoh*
…caravan site?	…campeggio per camper? *kampedjoh pehr kamper*
Can we camp here?	Possiamo accamparci qui? *possyamoh akamparchee kwee*
Do you have any vacancies?	C'è posto disponibile? *che postoh deesponeebeeleh*
What is the charge…	Quanto costa… *kwantoh kostah*
…per night?	…per notte? *pehr notteh*
…per week?	…per settimana? *pehr setteemanah*
Does the price include…	Il costo include… *eel kostoh eenkloodeh*
…electricity?	…l'elettricità? *leletreecheetah*
…hot water?	…l'acqua calda? *lakwa kaldah*
We want to stay for…	Desideriamo rimanere per… *deseederyamoh reemanereh pehr*

il picchetto
eel peekkettoh
tent peg

la tenda
lah tendah
tent

la corda
lah kordah
guy rope

Can I rent…	Posso noleggiare… *possoh noledjareh*
…a tent?	…una tenda? *oonah tendah*
…a barbecue?	…un barbecue? *oon barbecue*
Where are…	Dove sono… *doveh sonoh*
…the toilets?	…i servizi? *ee serveetsee*
…the dustbins?	…i bidoni dell'immondizia? *ee beedonee del eemondeetsya*
Are there…	Ci sono… *chee sonoh*
…showers?	…docce? *dotcheh*
…laundry facilities?	…servizi di lavanderia? *serveetsee dee lavanderya*
Is there…	C'è… *che*
…a swimming pool?	…una piscina? *oonah peesheenah*
…a shop?	…un negozio? *oon negotsyo*

You may hear…

- **Non accendere il fuoco.** *non atchendereh eel fwoko* Don't light a fire.

- **Non bere l'acqua.** *non bereh lakwa* Don't drink the water.

AT THE CAMPSITE

il sacco a pelo
eel sakko ah peloh
sleeping bag

il materasso gonfiabile
eel materassoh gonfyabeeleh
air mattress

il bollitore
eel boleetoreh
camping kettle

il thermos
eel termos
vacuum flask

il fornello da campeggio
eel fornelloh dah kampedjoh
camping stove

il barbecue
eel barbecue
barbecue

il frigo portatile
eel freegoh portateeleh
coolbox

l'acqua in bottiglia
lakwa een botteelya
bottled water

il cestino da picnic
eel chesteenoh dah picnic
picnic hamper

il secchio
eel sekyo
bucket

il maglio
eel malyo
mallet

la bussola
lah boosolah
compass

la torcia
lah torchya
torch

la matassa di spago
lah matassah dee spagoh
ball of string

il filtro solare
eel feeltroh solareh
sunscreen

i cerotti
ee cherotee
plaster

gli scarponi da montagna
lye skarponee dah montanya
walking boots

lo zaino
loh dzaeenoh
backpack

SHOPPING

As well as shopping malls, supermarkets and specialist shops, Italy has many picturesque open-air markets in town squares and high streets where you can buy food, clothes and even antiques relatively cheaply. Most shops are open between 8.30am and 12.30pm, and 3.30pm to 7.30pm from Tuesday to Saturday. However, many stores and food shops are shut on Monday mornings or all day Mondays.

IN THE STORE

I'm looking for…	Sto cercando… *stoh cherkandoh*
Do you have…?	Avete…? *aveteh*
I'm just looking	Sto solo guardando *stoh soloh gwardandoh*
I'm being served	Mi stanno già servendo *mee stannoh jah servendoh*
Do you have any more of these?	Ne avete ancora? *eh aveteh ankorah*
How much is this?	Quanto costa questo? *wantoh kostah kwestoh*
Have you anything cheaper?	Avete qualcosa di meno costoso? *aveteh kwalkosah dee menoh kostosoh*
I'll take this one	Prendo questo/a *prendoh kwestoh/ah*
Where can I pay?	Dove posso pagare? *doveh possoh pagareh*
I'll pay…	Desidero pagare… *deseederoh pagareh*
…in cash	…in contanti *een kontantee*
…by credit card	…con la carta di credito *kon lah kartah dee kredeetoh*
Can I have a receipt?	Mi può fare lo scontrino? *mee pwo fareh loh skontreenoh?*
I'd like to exchange this	Vorrei cambiare questo/a *vorray kambyareh kwestoh/ah*

IN THE BANK

I'd like…	Desidero… *deseederoh*
…to make a withdrawal	…effettuare un prelievo *effettwareh oon prelyevoh*
…to pay in some money	…effettuare un deposito *effettwareh oon deposeetoh*
…to change some money	…cambiare del denaro *kambyareh del denaroh*
…into euros	…in euro *een ehooroh*
…into sterling	…in sterline *een sterleeneh*
Here is my passport	Ecco il mio passaporto *ekko eel meeo passaportoh*
My name is…	Mi chiamo… *mee kiamoh*
My account number is…	Il mio numero di conto è… *eel meeo noomeroh dee kontoh eh*
My bank details are…	I miei dettagli bancari sono… *ee myayee dettalyee bankaree sonoh*

il tasso di cambio
eel tassoh dee kambyo
exchange rate

i travellers' cheque
ee travelers cheque
traveller's cheque

il passaporto
eel passaportoh
passport

il denaro
eel denaroh
money

Do I have...	Devo... *devoh*
...to key in my PIN?	...digitare il PIN? *deejeetareh eel peen*
...to sign here?	...firmare qui? *feermareh kwee*
The cash machine has eaten my card	Lo sportello bancomat ha preso la mia carta *loh sportelloh bankomat ah presoh lah meea kartah*
Can I cash a cheque?	Posso incassare un assegno? *possoh eenkassareh oon assenyo*
Has my money arrived yet?	È arrivato il mio denaro? *eh arreevatoh eel meeo denaroh*
When does the bank open/close?	Quando apre/chiude la banca? *kwandoh apreh/kewdeh lah bankah*

lo sportello bancomat
loh sportelloh bankomat
cash machine

il direttore della banca
eel deerettoreh dellah bankah
bank manager

la carta di credito
lah kartah dee kredeetoh
credit card

il libretto degli assegni
eel leebrettoh delyee assenyee
chequebook

SHOPS

la panetteria
lah panetterya
baker's

il fruttivendolo
eel frooteevendoloh
greengrocer's

la gastronomia
lah gastronomya
delicatessen

la pescheria
lah peskerya
fishmonger

il tabaccaio
eel tabakkayo
tobacconist

la boutique
lah booteek
boutique

il negozio di dischi
eel negotsyo dee deeskee
record shop

il negozio di mobili
eel negotsyo dee mobeelee
furniture shop

la macelleria
lah machelerya
butcher's

la drogheria
lah drogerya
grocer's

il supermercato
eel soopermerkatoh
supermarket

la libreria
lah leebrerya
book shop

il negozio di calzature
eel negotsyo dee kaltsatooreh
shoe shop

la sartoria
lah sartorya
tailor's

la gioielleria
lah joyellerya
jeweller's

la ferramenta
lah ferramentah
hardware shop

AT THE MARKET

I would like...	Desidero... *deseederoh*
How much is this?	Quanto costa? *kwantoh kostah*
What's the price per kilo?	Quanto costa al chilo? *kwantoh kostah al keeloh*
It's too expensive	È troppo caro *eh troppoh karoh*
Do you have anything cheaper?	Avete qualcosa di meno caro? *aveteh kwalkosah dee menoh karoh*
That's fine, I'll take it	Va bene, lo prendo *vah beneh loh prendoh*
I'll take two kilos	Me ne dia due chili *meh neh dya dooeh keelee*
A kilo of...	Un chilo di... *oon keeloh dee*
Half a kilo of...	Mezzo chilo di... *medzo keeloh dee*
A little more, please	Un po' di più, per favore *oon poh dee pew pehr favoreh*
May I taste it?	Posso assaggiarlo/a? *possoh assadjarloh/ah*
That will be all, thank you	È tutto, la ringrazio *eh tootoh lah reengratsyo*

You may hear...

- **Posso aiutarla?**
  possoh ayewtarlah
  Can I help you?

- **Quanto ne vuole?**
  kwantoh neh vwoleh
  How much would you like?

IN THE SUPERMARKET

Where is/are...	Dov'è/dove sono... *doveh/doveh sonoh*
...the frozen foods	...i surgelati? *ee soorjelatee*
...the drinks aisle?	...la corsia delle bibite? *lah korsya delleh beebeeteh*
...the check-out?	...la cassa? *lah kassah*

il carrello
eel karrelloh
trolley

il cestino
eel chesteenoh
basket

I'm looking for...	Sto cercando... *stoh cherkandoh*
Do you have any more?	Ne avete ancora? *neh aveteh ankorah*
Is this reduced?	È scontato? *eh skontatoh*
What is the sell-by date?	Qual è la data di scadenza? *kwaleh lah datah dee skadentsa*
Where do I pay?	Dove posso pagare? *doveh possoh pagareh*
Shall I key in my PIN?	Devo digitare il PIN? *devoh deejeetareh eel peen*
Can I have a bag?	Posso avere un sacchetto? *possoh avereh oon sakettoh*
Can you help me pack	Mi può aiutare a riempire i sacchetti? *mee pwo ayewtareh ah ryempeereh ee sakettee*

FRUIT

l'arancia
laranchya
orange

il limone
eel leemoneh
lemon

il limone verde
eel leemoneh verdeh
lime

il pompelmo
eel pompelmoh
grapefruit

la pesca
lah peskah
peach

la pescanoce
lah peskanocheh
nectarine

l'albicocca
lalbeekokkah
apricot

la prugna
lah proonya
plum

la ciliegia
lah cheelyeja
cherry

il mirtillo
eel meerteeloh
blueberry

la fragola
lah fragolah
strawberry

il lampone
eel lamponeh
raspberry

il melone
eel meloneh
melon

l'uva
loovah
grapes

la banana
lah bananah
banana

la melagrana
lah melagranah
pomegranate

la mela
lah melah
apple

la pera
lah perah
pear

l'ananas
lananas
pineapple

il mango
eel mangoh
mango

VEGETABLES

la patata
lah patatah
potato

la carota
lah karotah
carrot

il peperone
eel peperoneh
pepper

il peperoncino
eel peperoncheenoh
chilli

la melanzana
lah melandzanah
aubergine

il pomodoro
eel pomodoroh
tomato

la cipollina
lah cheepoleenah
spring onion

il porro
eel porroh
leek

la cipolla
lah cheepolah
onion

l'aglio
lalyo
garlic

il fungo
eel foongoh
mushroom

la zucchina
lah dzookeenah
courgette

il cetriolo
eel chetryoloh
cucumber

i fagiolini
ee fajoleenee
French bean

i piselli
ee peesellee
garden peas

il sedano
eel sedanoh
celery

gli spinaci
lyee speenachee
spinach

il broccolo
eel brokkoloh
broccoli

il cavolo
eel kavoloh
cabbage

la lattuga
lah latoogah
lettuce

MEAT AND POULTRY

May I have...	Posso avere... *possoh avereh*
...a slice of...?	...una fetta di...? *oonah fettah dee*
...a piece of...?	...un pezzo di...? *oon pedzo dee*

il prosciutto cotto
eel proshewtoh kottoh
cooked ham

il prosciutto crudo
eel proshewtoh kroodoh
cured ham

la bistecca
lah beestekka
steak

il filetto
eel feelettoh
fillet

il salame di cinghiale
eel salameh dee cheengyaleh
wild boar salami

la carne tritata
lah karneh treetatah
mince

il pollo
eel polloh
chicken

il rognone
eel ronyoneh
kidney

FISH AND SHELLFISH

la sogliola
lah solyolah
sole

eel calamaro
eel kalamaroh
squid

il merluzzo
eel merloodzo
cod

la spigola
lah speegolah
sea bass

il sarago
eel saragoh
sea bream

la sardina
lah sardeenah
sardine

il granchio
eel grankyo
crab

l'aragosta
laragostah
lobster

il gambero
eel gamberoh
prawn

la capasanta
lah kapasantah
scallop

BREAD AND CAKES

il panino
eel paneenoh
roll

il pan marino
eel pan mareenoh
rosemary bread

il pane casalingo
eel paneh kasaleengoh
household bread

i grissini
ee greeseenee
breadsticks

il cornetto
eel kornettoh
croissant

la focaccia
lah fokatchya
foccaccia

la crostata al limone
lah krostatah al leemoneh
lemon tart

la torta al cioccolato
lah tortah al chokolatoh
chocolate cake

il panettone
eel panettoneh
panettone

il panforte
eel panforteh
panforte

DAIRY PRODUCE

il latte intero
eel lateh eenteroh
whole milk

parzialmente scremato
partsyalmenteh skrematoh
semi-skimmed

la panna
lah pannah
single cream

la ricotta
lah reekottah
ricotta

lo yoghurt
loh yogoort
yoghurt

il burro
eel booroh
butter

il provolone
eel provoloneh
Provolone

il parmigiano
eel parmeejanoh
Parmesan cheese

la mozzarella
lah modzarellah
mozzarella

il pecorino
eel pekoreenoh
Pecorino

NEWSPAPERS AND MAGAZINES

Do you have...	Avete... *aveteh*
...a book of stamps?	...un carnet di francobolli? *oon karneh dee frankobollee*
...airmail stamps?	...francobolli di posta aerea? *frankobollee dee postah ahehrehah*
...a packet of envelopes?	...una confezione di buste? *oonah konfetsyoneh dee boosteh*

la cartolina
lah kartoleenah
postcard

i francobolli
ee frankobolee
stamps

la matita
lah mateetah
pencil

la penna
lah pennah
pen

You may hear...

- **Quale desidera?**
  kwaleh deseederah
  Which would you like?

- **Mi può dire la sua età?**
  mee pwo deereh lah sooa etah
  How old are you?

- **Ha la carta d'identità?**
  ah lah kartah deedenteetah
  Do you have ID?

I'd like…	Vorrei… *vorray*
…a pack of cigarettes	…un pacchetto di sigarette *oon pakkettoh dee seegaretteh*
…a box of matches	…una scatola di cerini *oonah skatolah dee chereenee*

del tabacco
del tabakkoh
tobacco

l'accendino
latchendeenoh
lighter

le gomme da masticare
leh gommeh dah masteekareh
chewing gum

le caramelle
leh karamelleh
sweets

il quotidiano
eel kwoteedyanoh
newspaper

la rivista
lah reeveestah
magazine

i fumetti
ee foomettee
comic

le matite colorate
leh mateeteh kolorateh
colouring pencils

BUYING CLOTHES

I am looking for…	Sto cercando… *stoh cherkandoh*
I am size…	Porto la taglia… *portoh lah talya*
Do you have this…	Avete questo/a… *aveteh kwestoh/ah*
…in my size?	…nella mia taglia? *nellah meeah talya*
…in small	…in taglia piccola? *een talya peekolah*
…in medium?	…in taglia media? *een talya medya*
…in large?	…in taglia grande? *een talya grandeh*
…in other colours?	…in altri colori? *een altree koloree*
Can I try this on?	Posso provarlo/a? *possoh provarloh/ah*
Where are the changing rooms?	Dove sono gli spogliatoi? *doveh sonoh lye spolyatoee*
It's…	È… *eh*
…too big	…troppo grande *troppoh grandeh*
…too small	…troppo piccolo/a *troppoh peekoloh/ah*
I need…	Ho bisogno di… *oh beezonyo dee*
…a larger size	…una taglia più grande *oonah talya pew grandeh*
…a smaller size	…una taglia più piccola *oonah talya pew peekolah*
I'll take this one, please	Prendo questo/a, grazie *prendoh kwestoh/ah gratsye*
Is this on sale?	È in saldo? *eh een saldoh*

BUYING SHOES

I take shoe size…	Mi serve un… *mee serveh oon*
Can I try…	Posso provare… *possoh provareh*
…this pair?	…questo paio? *kwestoh payo*
…those ones in the window?	…quelle in vetrina? *kwelleh een vetreenah*
These are…	Queste sono… *kwesteh sonoh*
…too tight	…troppo strette *troppoh stretteh*
…too big	…troppo larghe *troppoh largeh*
…too small	…troppo piccole *troppoh peekoleh*
…uncomfortable	…scomode *skomodeh*
Is there a bigger/ smaller size?	Avete un numero più grande/piccolo? *aveteh oon noomeroh pew grandeh/peekoloh*

Clothes and shoe sizes guide

Women's clothes sizes

UK	6	8	10	12	14	16	18	20
Europe	34	36	38	40	42	44	46	48
USA	4	6	8	10	12	14	16	18

Men's clothes sizes

UK	36	38	40	42	44	46	48	50
Europe	46	48	50	52	54	56	58	60
USA	36	38	40	42	44	46	48	50

Women's shoes

UK	3	4	5	6	7	8	9
Europe	36	37	38	39	40	42	43
USA	5	6	7	8	9	10	11

CLOTHES AND SHOES

il vestito
eel vesteetoh
dress

l'abito da sera
labeetoh dah serah
evening dress

la giacca
lah jakkah
jacket

il maglione
eel malyoneh
jumper

i jeans
ee jeenz
jeans

la gonna
lah gonnah
skirt

la scarpa da ginnastica
lah skarpah dah jeennasteekah
trainer

lo stivale
loh steevaleh
boot

la borsa
lah borzah
handbag

la cintura
lah cheentoorah
belt

il vestito da uomo
eel vesteetoh dah womoh
suit

il cappotto
eel kapottoh
coat

la camicia
lah kameechya
shirt

la t-shirt
lah t-shirt
t-shirt

i calzoncini
ee kaltsoncheenee
shorts

la scarpa col tacco alto
lah skarpah kol takko altoh
high-heel shoe

la scarpa con lacci
lah skarpah kon latchee
lace-up shoe

il sandalo
eel sandaloh
sandal

l'infradito
leenfradeetoh
flip-flop

i calzini
ee kalseenee
socks

AT THE GIFT SHOP

I'd like to buy a gift for...	Vorrei acquistare un regalo per... *vorray akweestareh oon regaloh pehr*
...my mother/father	...mia madre/mio padre *meeah madreh/meeoh padreh*
...my daughter/son	...mia figlia/mio figlio *meeah feelya/meeoh feelyo*
...a child	...un/a bambino/a *oon/ah bambeenoh/ah*
...a friend	...un/a amico/a *oon/ah ameekoh/ah*
Can you recommend something?	Mi può consigliare qualcosa? *mee pwo konseelyareh kwalkosah*
Do you have a box for it?	Ha la scatola? *ah lah skatolah*
Can you gift-wrap it?	Può fare un pacchetto regalo? *pwo fareh oon pakettoh regaloh*

la collana
lah kollanah
necklace

il bracciale
eel bratchyaleh
bracelet

l'orologio
lorolojoh
watch

i gemelli
ee jemellee
cufflinks

la bambola
lah bambolah
doll

il peluche
eel peloosh
soft toy

il portafoglio
eel portafolyo
wallet

i cioccolatini
ee chokolateenee
chocolates

I want a souvenir of…	Desidero un souvenir di… *deseederoh oon soovenir dee*
Have you anything cheaper?	Ha qualcosa di meno caro? *ah kwalkosah dee menoh karoh*
Is there a guarantee?	È coperto/a da garanzia? *eh kopertoh/ah dah garantsya*

You may hear…

- **È un regalo?**
  eh oon regaloh
  Is it a present?

- **Vuole un pacchetto regalo?**
  vwoleh oon pakettoh regaloh
  Shall I gift-wrap it?

PHOTOGRAPHY

I'd like this film developed	Vorrei sviluppare questa pellicola *vorray sveeloopareh kwestah pelleekolah*
Do you have an express service?	Avete un servizio espresso? *aveteh oon serveetsyo espressoh*
Does it cost more?	Costa di più? *kostah dee pew*
I'd like...	Vorrei... *vorray*
...the one-hour service	...lo sviluppo in un'ora *loh sveeloopoh een oonorah*
...a battery	...una batteria *oonah battereeya*

la fotocamera digitale
lah fotokamerah deejeetaleh
digital camera

la scheda di memoria
lah skedah dee memorya
memory card

il rullino
eel rooleenoh
roll of film

l'album delle fotografie
lalboom delleh fotografye
photo album

la cornice
lah korneeche
photo frame

Do you print digital photos?

Stampate le fotografie digitali?
stampateh leh fotografye deejeetalee

Can you print from this memory stick?

Potete stampare da questa chiavetta USB?
poteteh stampareh dah kwestah kyakettah oo-es-bee

il flash
eel flash
flash gun

la fotocamera
lah fotokamerah
camera

gli obiettivi
lyee obyeteevee
lens

la borsa per fotocamera
lah borsah pehr fotokamerah
camera bag

You may hear...

- Quale formato di foto desidera?
  kwaleh formatoh deseedeerah?
  What size prints do you want?

- Opache o lucide?
  opakeh oh loocheedeh?
  Matt or gloss?

AT THE POST OFFICE

I'd like…	Vorrei… *vorray*
…three stamps, please	…tre francobolli, per favore *treh frankobollee pehr favoreh*
…to register this letter	…inviare una raccomandata *eenvyareh oonah rakomandatah*
…to send this airmail	…inviare questo per posta aerea *eenvyareh kwestoh pehr postah ahehreha*

la busta
lah boostah
envelope

i francobolli
ee frankobollee
stamps

la cartolina
lah kartoleenah
postcard

la posta aerea
lah postah ahehreha
airmail

You may hear…

- **Cosa contiene?**
  kozah kontyeneh
  What are the contents?

- **Qual è il suo valore?**
  kwaleh eel soo-oh valoreh
  What is their value?

- **Riempia questo modulo.**
  ryempya kwestoh modooloh
  Fill out this form.

How much is…?	Quanto costa… *kwantoh kostah*
…a letter to…	…una lettera per… *oonah letterah pehr*
…a postcard to…	…una cartolina per… *oonah kartoleenah pehr*
…Great Britain	…la Gran Bretagna *lah gran bretanya*

il pacco
eel pakoh
parcel

il corriere
eel korryereh
courier

la cassetta delle lettere
lah kassettah delleh lettereh
postbox

il postino
eel posteenoh
postman

…the United States	…gli Stati Uniti *lyee statee ooneetee*
…Canada	…il Canada *eel kanadah*
…Australia	…l'Australia *lowstralya*
Can I have a receipt?	Posso avere la ricevuta? *possoh avereh lah reechevootah*
Where can I post this?	Dove posso imbucare questa lettera? *doveh possoh eembookareh kwestah letterah*

TELEPHONES

Where is the nearest phone box?

Dov'è la cabina telefonica più vicina?
doveh lah kabeenah telefoneekah pew veecheenah

il telefono
eel telefonoh
phone

il cellulare
eel chelloolareh
mobile phone

la scheda telefonica
lah skedah telefoneekah
phone card

la cabina telefonica
lah kabeenah telefoneekah
telephone box

il telefono a moneta
eel telefonoh ah monetah
coin phone

la segreteria telefonica
lah segreterya telefoneekah
answering machine

Who's speaking?	Pronto, chi parla? *prontoh kee parlah*
Hello, this is…	Pronto, sono… *prontoh sonoh*
I'd like to speak to…	Vorrei parlare con… *vorray parlareh kon*

INTERNET

Is there an internet café near here?	C'è un Internet cafè qui vicino? *che oon eenternet kafeh kwee veecheenoh*
How much do you charge?	Quanto costa? *kwantoh kostah*
Do you have wireless internet?	Avete un sistema Internet wireless? *aveteh oon seestemah eenternet wireless*
Can I check my emails?	Posso controllare le mie e-mail? *possoh kontrollareh leh meeyeh emayl*
I need to send an email	Devo inviare un'e-mail *devoh eenvyareh oonemayl*
What's your email address?	Qual è il suo indirizzo e-mail? *kwaleh eel soo-oh eendeereedzo emayl*
My email address is…	Il mio indirizzo e-mail è… *eel meeoh eendeereedzo emayl eh*

il computer portatile
eel compewter portateeleh
laptop

la tastiera
lah tastyerah
keyboard

il sito Web
eel seetoh web
website

l'e-mail
lemayl
email

SIGHTSEEING

Most Italian cities and towns have a tourist
information office, which is usually situated near
the railway station or town hall. The staff will
advise you on local places of interest to visit.
In Italy, most national museums close on Mondays
as well as on public holidays, so make sure that
you check the opening times before visiting.

AT THE TOURIST OFFICE

Where is the tourist information office?	Dov'è l'ufficio del turismo? *doveh loofeechyo del tooreesmoh*
Can you recommend...	Può consigliarmi... *pwo konseelyarmee*
...a guided tour?	...una visita guidata? *oonah veeseetah gweedatah*
...an excursion?	...una gita? *oonah jeetah*
Is there a museum or art gallery?	C'è un museo o una galleria d'arte? *che oon moozeoh oh oonah gallereeya darteh*
Is it open to the public?	È aperto/a al pubblico? *eh apertoh/ah al poobleekoh*
Is there wheelchair access?	C'è un accesso per disabili? *che oon atchessoh pehr deezabeelee*
Does it close...	È chiuso/a... *eh kewsoh/ah*
...on Sundays?	...la domenica? *lah domeneekah*
...on bank holidays?	...nei giorni festivi? *nay jornee festeevee*
How long does it take to get there?	Quanto ci vuole per arrivarci? *kwantoh chee vwoleh pehr areevarchee*
Do you have...	Avete... *aveteh*
...a street map?	...una cartina? *oonah karteenah*
...a guide?	...una guida? *oonah gweedah*
...any leaflets?	...degli opuscoli? *dehlyee opooskolee*

VISITING PLACES

What time…	A che ora… *ah ke orah*
…do you open?	…apre? *apreh*
…do you close?	…chiude? *kewdeh*
I'd like two entrance tickets	Vorrei due biglietti d'entrata *vorray dooeh beelyettee dentratah*
Two adults, please	Due adulti, per favore *dooeh adooltee pehr favoreh*
A family ticket	Un biglietto famiglia *oon beelyettoh fameelya*
How much does it cost?	Quanto costa? *kwantoh kostah*
Are there reductions for…	Ci sono delle riduzioni per… *chee sonoh delleh reedootsyonee pehr*
…children?	…i bambini? *ee bambeenee*
…students?	…gli studenti? *lyee stoodentee*

la pianta della città
lah pyantah dellah cheetah
street map

l'ufficio del turismo
loofeechyo del tooreesmoh
tourist office

il biglietto d'entrata
eel beelyettoh dentratah
entrance ticket

l'accesso disabili
latchessoh deezabeelee
wheelchair access

Can I buy a guidebook?	Posso acquistare una guida? *possoh akweestareh oonah gweedah*
Is there...	C'è... *che*
...an audio-guide?	...un'audio guida? *oonowdyo gweedah*
...a guided tour?	...una visita guidata? *oonah veeseetah gweedatah*
...a lift?	...un ascensore? *oon ashenzoreh*
...a bus tour?	...un giro turistico in autobus? *oon jeeroh tooreesteeko een owtoboos*
When is the next tour?	Quando parte il prossimo giro turistico? *kwandoh parteh eel proseemoh jeeroh tooreesteeko*

il tour in autobus
eel tour een owtoboos
tour bus

You may hear...

• **Possiede una carta studenti?**
possyedeh oonah kartah stoodentee
Do you have a student card?

• **Quanti anni ha?**
kwantee annee ah
How old are you?

FINDING YOUR WAY

Excuse me	Mi scusi *mee skoozee*
Can you help me?	Mi può aiutare? *mee pwo ayewtareh*
Is this the way to…?	È questa la strada per…? *eh kwestah lah stradah pehr*
How do I get to…?	Come raggiungo…? *komeh rajewngoh*
…the town centre?	…il centro della città? *eel chentroh dellah cheetah*
…the station?	…la stazione? *lah statsyoneh*
…the museum?	…il museo? *eel moozeoh*
…the art gallery?	…la galleria d'arte? *lah gallereeya darteh*
How long does it take?	Quanto tempo s'impiega? *kwantoh tempoh seempyegah*
Is it far?	È lontano? *eh lontanoh*
Can you show me on the map?	Me lo può indicare sulla cartina? *meh loh pwo eendeekareh soolah karteenah*

You may hear…

- **Non è lontano.** *non eh lontanoh* It's not far away.

- **Ci vogliono dieci minuti.** *chee volyonoh deeaychee meenootee* It takes ten minutes.

You may hear...

- **Siamo qui**
  syamoh kwee

  We are here

- **Vada sempre dritto...**
  vadah sempreh dreetoh

  Keep straight on...

- **...fino alla fine della via**
  feenoh allah feeneh dellah veeya

  ...to the end of the street

- **...fino al semaforo**
  feenoh al semaforoh

  ...to the traffic lights

- **...fino alla piazza principale**
  feenoh allah pyadza preencheepaleh

  ...to the main square

- **Di qua**
  dee kwa

  This way

- **Di là**
  dee lah

  That way

- **Svolti a destra al/alla...**
  svoltee ah destrah al/allah

  Turn right at...

- **Svolti a sinistra al/alla...**
  svoltee ah seeneestrah al/allah

  Turn left at...

- **Prenda la prima...**
  prendah lah preemah

  Take the first...

- **...a sinistra/a destra**
  ah seeneestrah/ah destrah

  ...on the left/right

- **È davanti a lei**
  eh davantee ah lay

  It's in front of you

- **È dietro di lei**
  eh deeyehtroh dee lay

  It's behind you

- **È di fronte a lei**
  eh dee fronteh ah lay

  It's opposite you

- **È vicino a...**
  eh veecheenoh ah

  It's next to...

- **C'è un'indicazione**
  che ooneendeekatsyoneh

  It's signposted

- **È là**
  eh lah

  It's over there

PLACES TO VISIT

il municipio
eel mooneecheepyo
town hall

il ponte
eel ponteh
bridge

il museo
eel moozeoh
museum

la galleria d'arte
lah gallereeya darteh
art gallery

il monumento
eel monoomentoh
monument

la chiesa
lah kyezah
church

la cattedrale
lah katedraleh
cathedral

il paese
eel paheseh
village

il parco
eel parkoh
park

il porto
eel portoh
harbour

il faro
eel faroh
lighthouse

il vigneto
eel veenyetoh
vineyard

il castello
eel kastelloh
castle

la costa
lah kostah
coast

la cascata
lah kaskatah
waterfall

le montagne
leh montanye
mountains

OUTDOOR ACTIVITIES

Where can we go...	Dove possiamo... *doveh possyamoh*
...horse riding?	...andare a cavallo? *andareh ah kavalloh*
...fishing?	...andare a pescare? *andareh ah peskareh*
...swimming?	...nuotare? *nwotareh*
...walking?	...fare un'escursione a piedi? *fareh oon eskoorzyoneh ah pyedee*
Can we...	Possiamo... *possyamoh*
...hire equipment?	...noleggiare l'attrezzatura? *noledjareh lattredzatoorah*
...have lessons?	...prendere delle lezioni? *prendereh delleh letsyonee*
How much per hour?	Quanto costa all'ora? *kwantoh kostah allorah*
I'm a beginner	Sono un/a principiante *sonoh oon/ah preencheepyanteh*
I'm quite experienced	Ho una buona esperienza *Oh oonah bwonah esperyentsah*
Where's the amusement park?	Dov'è il parco dei divertimenti? *doveh eel parkoh day deeverteementee*
Can the children go on all the rides?	I bambini possono andare su tutte le giostre? *ee bambeenee possonoh andareh soo tooteh leh jostreh*
Is there a playground?	C'è un'area giochi? *che oon ahrehah jokee*
Is it safe for children?	È sicura per i bambini? *eh seekoorah pehr ee bambeenee*

il luna park
eel loonah park
fairground

il parco a tema
eel parkoh ah temah
theme park

il parco safari
eel parkoh safaree
safari park

lo zoo
loh dzoh
zoo

l'area giochi
larehah jokee
playground

il picnic
eel picnic
picnic

pescare
peskareh
fishing

andare a cavallo
andareh ah kavalloh
horse riding

SPORTS AND LEISURE

Italy can offer the traveller a wide range of cultural events, entertainments, leisure activities and sports. The Italians are proud of their rich artistic and musical heritage, and their distinctive culture is very important to them. For the sports enthusiast, a wide range of spectator sports and facilities are available, from winter sports, climbing and hiking in the Alps and Appenines to watersports around the coast and on inland lakes. Football is the national game and you can watch a *Serie A* match.

LEISURE TIME

I like...	Mi piace/piacciono... *mee pyaceh/pyatchyonoh*
...art and painting	...l'arte e la pittura *larteh eh lah peetoorah*
...films and cinema	...i film e il cinema *ee film eh eel cheenemah*
...the theatre	...il teatro *eel tehatroh*
...opera	...l'opera *loperah*
I prefer...	Preferisco... *prefereeskoh*
...reading books	...leggere libri *ledjereh leebree*
...listening to music	...ascoltare musica *askoltareh moozeekah*
...watching sport	...guardare lo sport *gwardareh loh sport*
...playing games	...giocare a qualcosa *jokareh ah kwalkosah*
...going to concerts	...andare ai concerti *andareh ahee konchertee*
...dancing	...ballare *ballareh*
...going clubbing	...andare in discoteca *andareh een deeskotekah*
...going out with friends	...uscire con gli amici *oosheereh kon lyee ameechee*
I don't like...	Non mi piace... *non mee pyacheh*
That bores me	Mi annoia *mee annoyah*
That doesn't interest me	Non mi interessa *non mee eenteressah*

AT THE BEACH

Can I hire...	Posso noleggiare... *possoh noledjareh*
...a jet ski?	...una moto d'acqua? *oonah motoh dakwa*
...a beach umbrella?	...un ombrellone da mare? *oon ombrelloneh dah mareh*
...a surfboard?	...una tavola da surf? *oonah tavolah dah surf*
...a wetsuit?	...una muta subacquea? *oonah mootah soobakweah*

il telo da mare
eel teloh dah mareh
beach towel

il pallone da spiaggia
eel palloneh dah speeadjah
beach ball

la sedia a sdraio
lah sedya ah sdrayo
deck chair

il lettino sdraio
eel leteenoh sdrayo
sun lounger

You may hear...

- **Divieto di balneazione.**
deevyetoh dee balneatsyoneh
No swimming

- **Spiaggia chiusa.**
speeadja kewsah
Beach closed

gli occhiali da sole
lyee okeealee dah soleh
sunglasses

il cappello da sole
eel kappeloh dah soleh
sunhat

il bikini
eel beekeenee
bikini

la lozione solare
lah lotsyoneh solareh
suntan lotion

le pinne
leh peenneh
flippers

la maschera e il boccaglio
lah maskerah eh eel bokalyo
mask and snorkel

How much does it cost?	Quanto costa? *kwantoh kostah*
Can I go water-skiing?	Posso fare dello sci d'acqua? *possoh fareh delloh shee dakwa*
Is there a lifeguard?	C'è il bagnino? *che eel baneenoh*
Is it safe to…	È sicuro… *eh seekooroh*
…swim here?	…nuotare qui? *nwotareh kwee*
…surf here?	…fare del surf qui? *fareh del surf kwee*

AT THE SWIMMING POOL

What time...	Quando... *kwandoh*
...does the pool open?	...apre la piscina? *apreh lah peesheenah*
...does the pool close?	...chiude la piscina? *kewdeh lah peesheenah*
Is it...	È... *eh*
...an indoor pool?	...una piscina coperta? *oonah peesheenah kopertah*
...an outdoor pool?	...una piscina all'aperto? *oonah peesheenah alapertoh*
Is there a children's pool?	C'è una piscina per bambini? *che oonah peesheenah pehr bambeenee*
Where are the changing rooms?	Dove sono gli spogliatoi? *doveh sonoh lyee spolyatoy*
Is it safe to dive?	È sicuro tuffarsi? *eh seekooroh toofarsee*

i braccioli
ee bratchyolee
armband

la tavoletta
lah tavolettah
float

gli occhialini
lyee okyaleenee
swimming goggles

il costume
eel kostoomeh
swimsuit

AT THE GYM

il vogatore
eel vogatoreh
rowing machine

l'ellittica
lelleeteekah
cross trainer

la step machine
lah step machine
step machine

la bicicletta
lah beecheeklettah
exercise bike

Is there a gym?	C'è una palestra? *che oonah palestrah*
Is it free for guests?	È gratuita per i clienti? *eh gratooeetah pehr ee klyentee*
Do I have to wear trainers?	Devo indossare le scarpe da ginnastica? *devoh eendossareh leh skarpeh dah jeennasteekah*
Do I need an induction session?	Devo fare una sessione introduttiva? *devoh fareh oonah sessyoneh introdootteevah*
Do you hold...	Offrite... *offreeteh*
...aerobics classes?	...lezioni di aerobica? *letsyonee dee aerobeekah*
...Pilates classes?	...lezioni di Pilates? *letsyonee dee pilates*
...yoga classes?	...lezioni di yoga? *letsyonee dee yogah*

BOATING AND SAILING

Can I hire...	Posso noleggiare... *possoh noledjareh*
...a dinghy?	...un gommone? *oon gommoneh*
...a windsurfer?	...una tavola da windsurf? *oonah tavolah dah windsurf*
...a canoe?	...una canoa? *oonah kanoah*

il giubbotto di salvataggio
eel jewbottoh dee salvatadjoh
life jacket

la bussola
lah boosolah
compass

Do you offer sailing lessons?	Offrite lezioni di vela? *offreeteh letsyonee dee velah*
Do you have a mooring?	Avete un ormeggio? *aveteh oon ormedjoh*
How much is it for the night?	Quanto costa per notte? *kwantoh kostah pehr notteh*
Where can I buy gas?	Dove posso acquistare del gasolio? *doveh possoh akweestareh del gazolyo*
Where is the marina?	Dov'è il porticciolo? *doveh eel porteetchyoloh*
My...is broken	Il mio/la mia...non funziona *eel meeoh/lah meeah...non foontsyonah*
Can you repair it?	Potete ripararlo/a? *poteteh reepararloh/ah*
Are there life jackets?	Ci sono dei giubbotti di salvataggio? *chee sonoh day jewbottee dee salvatadjoh*

WINTER SPORTS

I would like to hire...	Desidero noleggiare... *deseederoh noledjareh*
...some skis	...un paio di sci *oon payo dee shee*
...some ski boots	...un paio di scarponi *oon payo dee skarponee*
...some poles	...un paio di racchette *oon payo dee raketteh*
...a snowboard	...uno snowboard *oonoh snowboard*
...a helmet	...un casco *oon kaskoh*
When does...	Quando... *kwandoh*
...the chair lift start?	...apre la seggiovia? *apreh lah sedjoveeya*
...the cable car finish?	...chiude la funivia? *kewdeh lah fooneeveeya*
How much is a lift pass?	Quanto costa un pass? *kwantoh kostah oon pass*
Can I take skiing lessons?	Posso prendere delle lezioni di sci? *possoh prendereh delleh letsyonee dee shee*

You may hear...

• È un principiante?
eh oon preencheepeeanteh
Are you a beginner?

• Deve lasciare un deposito.
deveh lashyareh oon deposeetoh
I need a deposit.

BALL GAMES

I like playing…	Mi piace giocare a… *mee pyacheh jokareh ah*
…football	…pallone *palloneh*
…tennis	…tennis *tennis*
…golf	…golf *golf*
…badminton	…volano *volahnoh*
…squash	…squash *skwosh*
…baseball	…baseball *besboll*
Where is the nearest…	Dov'è il più vicino… *doveh eel pew veecheenoh*
…tennis court?	…campo da tennis? *kampoh dah tennis*
…golf course?	…campo da golf? *kampoh dah golf*
…sports centre?	…centro sportivo? *chentroh sporteevoh*

il pallone
eel palloneh
football

i polsini
ee polseenee
wristbands

il canestro
eel kanestroh
basket

il guanto da baseball
eel gwantoh dah besball
baseball mitt

Can I book a court…	Posso prenotare un campo…
	possoh prenotareh oon kampoh
…for two hours?	…per due ore?
	pehr dooeh oreh
…at three o'clock?	…per le tre?
	pehr leh tray
What shoes are allowed?	Quali scarpe sono permesse?
	kwalee skarpeh sonoh permesseh
Can I hire…	Posso noleggiare…
	possoh noledjareh
…a tennis racquet?	…una racchetta da tennis?
	oonah rakettah dah tennis
…some balls?	…delle palle?
	delleh palleh
…a set of clubs?	…un set di mazze?
	oon set dee madze
…a golf buggy?	…il carrello elettrico?
	eel karreloh elettreekoh

la racchetta
lah rakettah
tennis racquet

le palle
leh palleh
tennis balls

la palla e il tee
lah pallah eh eel tee
golf ball and tee

la mazza
lah madza
golf club

GOING OUT

Where is…	Dov'è… *doveh*
…the opera house?	…il teatro dell'opera? *eel teatroh delloperah*
…a jazz club?	…il jazz club? *eel jazz clab*
Do I have to book in advance?	Devo prenotare in anticipo? *devoh prenotareh een anteecheepoh*
I'd like…tickets	Vorrei…biglietti *vorray…beelyettee*
I'd like seats…	Vorrei dei posti… *vorray day postee*
…at the back	…in fondo *een fondoh*
…at the front	…davanti *davantee*
…in the middle	…nel mezzo *nel medzo*
…in the gallery	…in galleria *een gallereeya*
Can I buy a programme?	Posso acquistare un programma? *possoh akweestareh oon programmah*
Is there live music?	C'è musica dal vivo? *che moozeekah dal veevoh*

You may hear…

- **Spenga il cellulare.**
  spengah eel chelloolareh
  Turn off your mobile.

- **Torni a sedere.**
  tornee ah sedereh
  Return to your seats.

il teatro
eel teatroh
theatre

il teatro dell'opera
eel teatroh delloperah
opera house

il musicista
eel moozeecheestah
musician

il pianista
eel pyaneestah
pianist

il/la cantante
eel/lah kantanteh
singer

la danza
lah dandza
ballet

il cinema
eel cheenemah
cinema

i popcorn
ee popcorn
popcorn

il casinò
eel kaseenoh
casino

il nightclub
eel naitklab
nightclub

GALLERIES AND MUSEUMS

What are the opening hours?	Qual è l'orario di apertura? *kwaleh loraryo dapertoorah*
Are there guided tours in English?	Ci sono delle visite guidate in inglese? *chee sonoh delleh veezeeteh gweedateh een eengleseh*
When does the tour leave?	Quando inizia la visita? *kwandoh eeneetsya lah veeseetah*
How much does it cost?	Quanto costa? *kwantoh kostah*
How long does it take?	Quanto dura? *kwantoh doorah*
Do you have an audio guide?	Avete delle guide audio? *aveteh delleh gweedeh owdyo*
Do you have a guidebook in English?	Avete una guida in inglese? *aveteh oonah gweedah een eengleseh*
Can you direct me to…?	Mi può indirizzare a…? *mee pwo eendeereetsareh ah*
Is (flash) photography allowed?	Sono permesse le fotografie (con il flash)? *sonoh permesseh leh fotografye (kon eel flash)*

la statua
lah statwa
statue

il busto
eel boostoh
bust

I'd really like to see…	Mi piacerebbe molto visitare… *mee pyacherebbeh moltoh veezeetareh*
Who painted this?	Chi è l'autore di questo quadro? *ki eh lowtoreh dee kwestoh kwadroh*
How old is it?	A quando risale? *ah kwandoh reesaleh*

il dipinto
eel deepeentoh
painting

l'incisione
leencheesyoneh
engraving

il disegno
eel deesenyo
drawing

il manoscritto
eel manoskreettoh
manuscript

Are there wheelchair ramps?	Ci sono delle rampe per disabili? *chee sonoh delleh rampeh pehr deezabeelee*
Is there a lift?	C'è un ascensore? *che oon ashenzoreh*
Where are the toilets?	Dov'è la toilette? *doveh lah twalet*
I've lost my group	Ho perso il mio gruppo *oh persoh eel meeoh grooppoh*

HOME ENTERTAINMENT

How do I…	Come… *komeh*
…turn the television on?	…accendo il televisore? *atchendoh eel televeezoreh*
…change channels?	…cambio i canali? *kambyo ee kanalee*
…turn the volume up?	…alzo il volume? *altso eel voloomeh*
…turn the volume down?	…abbasso il volume? *abassoh eel voloomeh*
Do you have satellite TV?	Avete una TV satellitare? *aveteh oonah TV satelleetareh*
Where can I buy…	Dove posso acquistare… *doveh possoh akweestareh*
…a DVD?	…un DVD? *oon deeveedee*
…a music CD?	…un CD musicale? *oon cheedee moozeekaleh*
…an audio CD?	…un CD audio? *oon cheedee owdyo*

il televisore a schermo panoramico
eel televeezoreh ah skermoh panorameekoh
widescreen TV

il lettore DVD
eel lettoreh deeveedee
DVD player

il telecomando
eel telekomandoh
remote control

il videogioco
eel videojokoh
video game

il lettore CD
eel lettoreh cheedee
CD player

l'iPod
lipod
iPod

la radio
lah radyo
radio

il portatile
eel portateeleh
laptop

il mouse
eel mows
mouse

Can I use this to…	Posso usarlo per… *possoh oozarloh pehr*
…go online?	…accedere ad Internet? *atchedereh ad eenternet*
Is it broadband/wifi?	È a banda larga/wifi? *eh ah bandah largah/wifi*
How do I…	Come… *komeh*
…log on?	…mi connetto? *mee konnettoh*
…log out?	…mi disconnetto? *mee deeskonnettoh*
…reboot?	…riavvio il computer? *reeyaveeyo eel compooter*

HEALTH

If you are an EU national, you are entitled to free emergency medical treatment in Italy, but you will have to produce your European Health Insurance Card. It is always a good idea to familiarize yourself with a few basic phrases for use in an emergency, or in case you need to go to a pharmacy, or visit a doctor, dentist or hospital

USEFUL PHRASES

I need a doctor	Ho bisogno di un medico *oh beezonyo dee oon medeekoh*
I would like an appointment…	Vorrei prendere un appuntamento… *vorray prendereh oon apoontamentoh*
…as soon as possible	…al più presto possibile *al pew prestoh posseebeeleh*
…today	…per oggi *pehr ojee*
…tomorrow	…per domani *pehr domanee*
It's very urgent	È molto urgente *eh moltoh oorjenteh*
I have a European Health Insurance Card	Possiedo una carta di assistenza sanitaria europea *possyedoh oonah kartah dee asseestentsa saneetarya ehoooropayah*
I have health insurance	Ho un'assicurazione sanitaria *oh oon asseekooratsyoneh saneetarya*
Can I have a receipt?	Posso avere la ricevuta? *possoh avereh lah reechevootah*
Where is the nearest…	Dov'è il più vicino/a… *doveh eel pew veecheenoh/ah*
…pharmacy?	…farmacia? *farmacheeya*
…doctor's surgery?	…ambulatorio medico? *amboolatoryo medeekoh*
…hospital?	…ospedale? *ospedaleh*
…dentist?	…dentista? *denteestah*

AT THE PHARMACY

What can I take for...?	Cosa posso prendere per...? *kozah possoh prendereh pehr*
How many should I take?	Quante ne devo prendere? *kwanteh neh devoh prendereh*
Is it safe for children?	È sicuro/a per i bambini? *eh seekooroh/ah pehr ee bambeenee*
Are there side effects?	Ha degli effetti indesiderati? *ah delyee effetee eendeseederatee*
Do you have that...	Questo prodotto viene venduto... *kwestoh prodottoh vyeneh vendootoh*
...as tablets?	...in compresse? *een kompresseh*
...in capsule form?	...in capsule? *een kapsooleh*
I'm allergic to...	Sono allergico/a a... *sonoh allerjeekoh/ah ah*
I'm already taking...	Sto già prendendo... *stoh jah prendendoh*
Do I need a prescription?	Ho bisogno della ricetta medica? *oh beezonyo dellah reechettah medeekah*

You may hear...

- Prenda questo/a... volte al giorno.
  prendah kwestoh/ah... volteh al jornoh
  Take this...times a day.

- Durante i pasti.
  dooranteh ee pastee
  With food.

le bende
leh bendeh
bandage

il cerotto
eel cherottoh
plaster

le capsule
leh kapsooleh
capsules

le compresse
leh compresseh
pills

l'inalatore
leenalatoreh
inhaler

le supposte
leh soopposteh
suppositories

le gocce
leh goccheh
drops

lo spray
loh spry
spray

la pomata
lah pomatah
ointment

lo sciroppo
loh sheeroppoh
syrup

THE HUMAN BODY

I have hurt my…

Mi sono fatto/a male
al/alla…
*mee sonoh fattoh/ah
maleh al/allah*

il gomito
eel gomeetoh
elbow

il braccio
eel bratchyo
arm

la testa
lah testah
head

la spalla
lah spallah
shoulder

il collo
eel kolloh
neck

il torace
eel torache
chest

lo stomaco
loh stomakoh
stomach

la gamba
lah gambah
leg

il ginocchio
eel jeenokyo
knee

il piede
eel pyedeh
foot

FACE

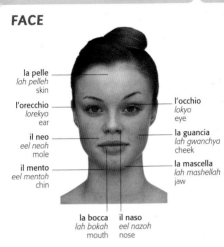

la pelle
lah pelleh
skin

l'orecchio
lorekyo
ear

il neo
eel neoh
mole

il mento
eel mentoh
chin

l'occhio
lokyo
eye

la guancia
lah gwanchya
cheek

la mascella
lah mashellah
jaw

la bocca
lah bokah
mouth

il naso
eel nazoh
nose

HAND   FOOT

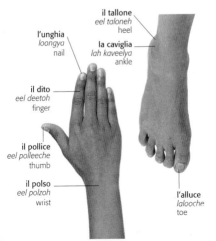

l'unghia
loongya
nail

il dito
eel deetoh
finger

il pollice
eel polleeche
thumb

il polso
eel polzoh
wrist

il tallone
eel taloneh
heel

la caviglia
lah kaveelya
ankle

l'alluce
lalooche
toe

FEELING ILL

I don't feel well	Non mi sento bene *non mee sentoh beneh*
I feel ill	Mi sento male *mee sentoh maleh*
I have...	Ho... *Oh*
...an ear ache	...mal d'orecchio *mal dorekyo*
...a stomach ache	...mal di stomaco *mal dee stomakoh*
...a sore throat	...la gola infiammata *lah golah enfyammatah*
...a temperature	...la febbre *lah febbreh*
...hayfever	...il raffreddore da fieno *eel rafreddoreh dah fyenoh*
...constipation	...costipazione *kosteepatsyoneh*
...diarrhoea	...diarrea *dyareah*
...toothache	...mal di denti *mal dee dentee*
I've been stung by...	Mi ha punto... *mee ah poontoh*
...a bee/wasp	...un'ape/una vespa *oonapeh/oonah vespah*
...a jellyfish	...una medusa *oonah medoosah*
I've been bitten by...	Mi ha morso... *mee ah morsoh*
...a snake	...un serpente *oon serpenteh*
...a dog	...un cane *oon kaneh*

INJURIES

il taglio
eel talyo
cut

l'escoriazione
leskoryatsyoneh
graze

l'ematoma
lematomah
bruise

la scheggia
lah skedjah
splinter

la scottatura solare
lah skotatoorah solareh
sunburn

la bruciatura
lah broochyatoorah
burn

il morso
eel morsoh
bite

la puntura
lah poontoorah
sting

la distorsione
lah deestorsyoneh
sprain

la frattura
lah fratoorah
fracture

AT THE DOCTOR

I'm...	Sto... *stoh*
...vomiting	...vomitando *vomeetandoh*
...bleeding	...perdendo sangue *perdendoh sangwe*
...dizzy	...ho le vertigini *oh leh verteejeenee*
...feeling faint	...mi sento svenire *mee sentoh sveneereh*
...pregnant	...sono incinta *sonoh eencheentah*
...diabetic	...ho il diabete *oh eel dyabeteh*
...epileptic	...sono epilettico/a *sonoh epeeletteekoh/ah*
I have...	Soffro di... *soffroh dee*
...arthritis	...artrite *artreeteh*
...a heart condition	...una patologia cardiaca *oonah patolojeea kardeeakah*
...high blood pressure	...elevata pressione sanguigna *elevatah pressyoneh sangweenya*

You may hear...

- Cosa c'è che non va?
  kozah che ke non vah
  What's wrong?

- Dove le fa male?
  doveh leh fah maleh
  Where does it hurt?

- Posso visitarla?
  possoh veezeetarlah
  Can I examine you?

ILLNESS

il mal di testa
eel mal dee testah
headache

il sangue dal naso
eel sangwe dal nasoh
nosebleed

la tosse
lah tosseh
cough

lo starnuto
loh starnootoh
sneeze

il raffreddore
eel rafreddoreh
cold

l'influenza
leenflooentsa
flu

l'asma
lasmah
asthma

i crampi
ee krampee
stomach cramps

la nausea
lah nowzeah
nausea

l'eruzione cutanea
lerootsyoneh kootaneah
rash

AT THE HOSPITAL

Can you help me?	Mi può aiutare? *mee pwo ayewtareh*
I need...	Ho bisogno di... *oh beezonyo dee*
...a doctor	...un dottore *oon dottoreh*
...a nurse	...un'infermiera *oon eenfermyerah*
Where is...	Dov'è... *doveh*
...the accident and emergency department?	...il Pronto Soccorso? *eel prontoh sokorzoh*
...the children's ward?	...il reparto pediatrico? *eel repartoh pedyatreeko*
...the X-ray department?	...il reparto di radiologia? *eel repartoh dee radyolojah*
...the lift/stairs?	...l'ascensore/la scala? *lashensoreh/lah skalah*
...the waiting room?	...la sala d'attesa? *lah salah dattesah*

l'iniezione
leenyetsyoneh
injection

le analisi del sangue
leh analeezee del sangwe
blood test

la radiografia
lah radyografya
X-ray

l'ecografia, la TAC
lekografya lah tac
scan

...the intensive care unit?	...il reparto di terapia intensiva? _eel repartoh dee terapya eentenzeevah_
I think I've broken...	Penso di essermi rotto/a... _pensoh dee essermee rottoh/ah_
Do I need...	Ho bisogno di... _oh beezonyo dee_
...an injection?	...un'iniezione? _ooneenyetsyoneh_
...an operation?	...un'operazione? _oonoperatsyoneh_
Will it hurt?	Sarà doloroso/a? _sarah dolorosoh/ah_
How long will it take?	Quanto tempo sarà necessario? _kwantoh tempoh sarah nechessaryo_
What are the visiting hours?	Quali sono gli orari di visita? _kwalee sonoh lyee oraree dee veeseetah_

la sedia a rotelle
lah sedya ah rotelleh
wheelchair

la rianimazione
lah reeaneematsyoneh
resuscitation

la stecca
lah stekkah
splint

la fasciatura
lah fashyatoorah
dressing

EMERGENCIES

In an emergency, you should dial 113 and ask for either an ambulance (*un ambulanza*), the fire brigade (*i vigili del fuoco*), the police (*la Polizia*) or the military police (*i Carabinieri*), which is part of the army. If you are the victim of a crime or lose your passport and money, you should report the incident to the police. In the following pages, you will find some useful phrases to help you.

IN AN EMERGENCY

Help!	Aiuto! *ayewtoh*
Please go away!	Mi lasci stare! *mee lashee stareh*
Let go!	Lasci! *lashee*
Stop! Thief!	Fermo! Al ladro! *fermoh al ladroh*
Call the police!	Chiamate la polizia! *kiamateh lah poleetseeya*
Get a doctor!	Trovate un dottore! *trovateh oon dottoreh*
I need...	Ho bisogno... *oh beezonyo*
...the police	...della polizia *dellah poleetseeya*
...the fire brigade	...dei vigili del fuoco *day veejeelee del fwoko*
...an ambulance	...di un'ambulanza *dee oon amboolantsa*
It's very urgent	È molto urgente *eh moltoh oorjenteh*
Where is...	Dov'è... *doveh*
...the British embassy?	...l'ambasciata britannica? *lambashyatah breetaneekah*
...the British consul?	...il console britannico? *eel konsoleh breetaneekoh*
...the police station?	...il commissariato? *eel komeesareeyatoh*
...the hospital?	...l'ospedale? *lospedaleh*

ACCIDENTS

I need to make a telephone call	Devo fare una telefonata *devoh fareh oonah telefonatah*
I'd like to report an accident	Vorrei denunciare un incidente *vorray denoonchyareh oon eencheedenteh*
I've crashed my car	Ho avuto un incidente d'auto *oh avootoh oon eencheedenteh dowtoh*
The registration number is...	Il numero di targa è... *eel noomeroh dee targah eh*
I'm at...	Mi trovo a/in... *mee trovoh ah/een*
Please come quickly!	Venite subito, per favore! *veneeteh soobeetoh pehr favoreh*
Someone's injured	Qualcuno è ferito *kwalkoonoh eh fereetoh*
Someone's been knocked down	Qualcuno è stato investito *kwalkoonoh eh statoh eenvesteetoh*
There's a fire at...	C'è un incendio a/in... *che oon eenchendyo ah/een*

You may hear...

- **Di quale servizio ha bisogno?**
  dee kwaleh serveetsyo ah beezonyo
  Which service do you require?

- **Cos'è successo?**
  kozeh sootchessoh
  What happened?

EMERGENCY SERVICES

l'ambulanza
lamboolantsa
ambulance

i vigili del fuoco
ee veejeelee del fwoko
firefighters

l'autopompa
lowtopompah
fire engine

l'allarme antincendio
lalarmeh anteenchendyo
fire alarm

l'idrante
leedranteh
hydrant

l'estintore
lesteentoreh
fire extinguisher

le manette
leh manetteh
handcuffs

la volante
lah volanteh
police car

il poliziotto
eel poleetsyottoh
policeman

POLICE AND CRIME

I want to report a crime	Desidero sporgere denuncia *deseederoh sporjereh denoonchya*
I've been...	Sono vittima... *sonoh veeteemah*
...robbed	...di un furto *dee oon foortoh*
...attacked	...di un attacco *dee oon attakko*
...mugged	...di un borseggio *dee oon borsejoh*
...raped	...di una violenza sessuale *dee oonah vyolentsa sessooaleh*
...burgled	...di un furto *dee oon foortoh*
Someone has stolen...	Qualcuno ha rubato... *kwalkoonoh ah roobatoh*
...my car	...la mia auto *lah meeah owtoh*
...my money	...il mio denaro *eel meeoh denaroh*
...my traveller's cheques	...i miei traveller's cheques *ee myeh-ee traveller's cheques*
...my passport	...il mio passaporto *eel meeoh passaportoh*

You may hear...

- Quando è successo? *kwandoh eh sootchessoh* When did it happen?

- Ci sono testimoni? *chee sonoh testeemonee* Was there a witness?

- Si ricorda l'aspetto? *see reekordah laspettoh* What did he look like?

I'd like to speak to…	Vorrei parlare con… *vorray parlareh kon*
…a senior officer	…un responsabile *oon responsabeeleh*
…a policewoman	…una poliziotta *oonah poleetsyottah*
I need…	Ho bisogno di… *oh beezonyo dee*
…a lawyer	…un avvocato *oon avokatoh*
…an interpreter	…un interprete *oon eenterpreteh*
…to make a phone call	…fare una telefonata *fareh oonah telefonatah*
I'm very sorry, officer	Mi spiace molto, signor agente *mee spyacheh moltoh seenyor ajenteh*
Here is…	Ecco… *ekko*
…my driving licence	…la patente *lah patenteh*
…my insurance	…l'assicurazione *lasseekooratsyoneh*
How much is the fine?	A quanto ammonta la multa? *ah kwantoh ammontah lah mooltah*

You may hear…

- Favorisca la patente per favore.
 favoreeska lah patenteh pehr favoreh
 Your licence please.

- Favoreeska i documenti.
 favoreeska ee dokementee
 Your papers.

AT THE GARAGE

Where is the nearest garage?	Dov'è la più vicina autofficina? *doveh lah pew veecheenah owtoffeecheenah*
Can you do repairs?	Effettuate le riparazioni? *effettwateh leh reeparatsyonee*
I need...	Ho bisogno di... *oh beezonyo dee*
...a new tyre	...un nuovo pneumatico *oon nwovoh pneoomateekoh*
...a new exhaust	...un nuovo tubo di scarico *oon nwovoh tooboh dee skareekoh*
...a new windscreen	...un nuovo parabrezza *oon nwovoh parabretsa*
...a new bulb	...una nuova lampadina *oonah nwovah lampadeenah*
...wiper blades	...spazzole del tergicristallo *spatsoleh del terjeekreestalloh*
Do you have one in stock?	Ne avete in magazzino? *neh aveteh een magadzeenoh*
Can you replace this?	Può sostituirlo/a? *pwo sosteetweerloh/ah*
The...is not working	Il/la...non funziona *eel/lah...non foontsyonah*
There is something wrong with the engine	Il motore non funziona bene *eel motoreh non foontsyonah beneh*
Is it serious?	È grave? *eh graveh*
When will it be ready?	Quando sarà pronta? *kwandoh sarah prontah*
How much will it cost?	Quanto costerà? *kwantoh kosterah*

CAR BREAKDOWN

My car has broken down	La mia automobile è in panne *lah meeah owtomobeeleh eh een panneh*
Please can you help me?	Mi può aiutare? *mee pwo ayewtareh*
Please come to...	Venga a... *vengah ah*
I have a puncture	Ho una gomma a terra *oh oonah gommah ah terrah*
Can you help change the wheel?	Mi può aiutare a cambiare la ruota? *mee pwo ayewtareh ah kambyareh lah rwotah*
I need a new tyre	Ho bisogno di un nuovo pneumatico *oh beezonyo dee oon nwovoh pneoomateekoh*
My car won't start	La mia auto non si accende *lah meeah owtoh non see atchendeh*
The engine is overheating	Il motore si sta surriscaldando *eel motoreh see stah sooreeskaldandoh*
Can you fix it?	Può aggiustarla? *pwo adjoostarlah*

You may hear...

- **Ha bisogno di aiuto?**
  ah beezonyo dee ayewtoh
  Do you need any help?

- **Qual è il problema?**
  kwaleh eel problemah
  What is the problem?

- **Ha la ruota di scorta?**
  ah lah rwotah dee skortah
  Do you have a spare tyre?

LOST PROPERTY

I've lost…	Ho smarrito… *oh smareetoh*
…my money	…il mio denaro *eel meeoh denaroh*
…my keys	…le chiavi *leh kyavee*
…my glasses	…gli occhiali *lyee okyalee*
My luggage is missing	Il mio bagaglio è smarrito *eel meeoh bagalyo eh smareetoh*
My suitcase has been damaged	La mia valigia è stata danneggiata *la meeah valeeja eh statah dannedjatah*

il portafoglio
eel portafolyoh
wallet

il portamonete
eel portamoneteh
purse

la valigetta
lah valeejettah
briefcase

la borsa
lah borsah
handbag

la valigia
lah valeejah
suitcase

il traveller's cheque
eel travellers cheque
traveller's cheque

la carta di credito
lah kartah dee kredeetoh
credit card

il passaporto
eel passaportoh
passport

la fotocamera
lah fotokamerah
camera

il cellulare
eel chelloolareh
mobile phone

I need to phone my insurance company	Devo telefonare alla mia agenzia assicurativa *devoh telefonareh allah meeah ajentsya asseekoorateevah*
Can I put a stop on my credit cards?	Posso bloccare le mie carte di credito? *possoh blokareh leh myeh karteh dee kredeetoh*
My name is…	Mi chiamo… *mee kyamoh*
My policy number is…	Il numero della polizza è… *eel noomeroh dellah poleedza eh*
My address is…	Il mio indirizzo è… *eel meeo eendeereedzo eh*
My contact number is…	Il mio numero di telefono è… *eel meeoh noomeroh dee telefono eh*
My email address is…	Il mio indirizzo e-mail è… *eel meeoh eendeereedzo emayl eh*

MENU GUIDE

This guide lists the most common terms you may encounter on Italian menus or when shopping for food. If you can't find an exact phrase, try looking up its component parts.

A

abbacchio alla romana Roman-style spring lamb
acciughe sott'olio anchovies in oil
aceto vinegar
acqua water
acqua minerale gassata sparkling mineral water
acqua minerale non gassata still mineral water
acqua naturale still mineral water, tap water
affettato misto variety of cold, sliced meats
affogato al caffè hot espresso on ice cream
aglio garlic
agnello lamb
albicocche apricots
al forno roast
amatriciana chopped bacon and tomato sauce
ananas pineapple
anatra duck
anatra all'arancia duck in orange sauce
anguilla in umido stewed eel
anguria watermelon
antipasti starters
antipasti misti mixed starters
aperitivo aperitif
aragosta lobster
arancia orange
aranciata orangeade; fresh orange juice
aringa herring
arrosto roast

arrosto di tacchino roast turkey
asparagi asparagus
avocado all'agro avocado with dressing

B

baccalà dried cod
baccalà alla vicentina Vicentine-style dried cod
bagnacauda vegetables (often raw) in a sauce of oil, garlic, and anchovy
Barbaresco dry red wine from Piedmont
Barbera dry red wine from Piedmont
Bardolino dry red wine from the Veneto region
Barolo dark, dry red wine from Piedmont
basilico basil
bavarese ice-cream cake; dessert made with cream
Bel Paese soft, white cheese
besciamella white sauce
bignè cream puff
birra beer
birra chiara light beer, lager
birra grande large beer
birra piccola small beer
birra scura dark beer
bistecca ai ferri grilled steak
bistecca (di manzo) steak
bolognese mince and tomato sauce
braciola di maiale pork steak
branzino al forno baked sea bass

brasato braised beef with herbs

bresaola dried, salted beef eaten with oil and lemon

brioche type of croissant

brodo clear broth

brodo vegetale clear vegetable broth

bucatini long tube pasta

budino pudding

burro butter

burro di acciughe anchovy butter

C

Caciotta tender, white cheese from Central Italy

caffè coffee

caffè corretto espresso with a dash of liqueur

caffè latte half coffee, half hot milk

caffè lungo weak espresso

caffè macchiato espresso with a dash of milk

caffè ristretto strong espresso

calamari in umido stewed squid

calamaro squid

calzone folded pizza with tomato and cheese

camomilla camomile tea

cannella cinnamon

cannelloni al forno baked pasta rolls filled with meat

cappuccino espresso with frothy milk sprinkled with cocoa powder

capretto al forno roast kid

carbonara sauce of egg, bacon, and cheese

carciofi artichokes

carciofini sott'olio baby artichokes in oil

carne meat

carote carrots

carpaccio finely sliced beef fillet with oil, lemon, and parmesan

carré di maiale al forno roast pork loin

cassata siciliana ice-cream cake with chocolate, glacé fruit, and ricotta

castagne chestnuts

cavoletti di Bruxelles Brussels sprouts

cavolfiore cauliflower

cavolo cabbage

cefalo grey mullet

cernia grouper (fish)

cetriolo cucumber

charlotte ice-cream cake with biscuits and fruit

Chianti dark red Tuscan wine

cicoria chicory

cicorino small chicory plants

ciliege cherries

cime di rapa sprouting broccoli

cioccolata chocolate

cioccolata calda hot chocolate

cipolle onions

cocktail di gamberetti shrimp cocktail

conchiglie alla marchigiana pasta shells in tomato sauce with ham, celery, carrot, and parsley

coniglio rabbit

coniglio in umido stewed rabbit

consommé clear broth

contorni vegetables

coperto cover charge

coppa cured neck of pork

costata alla fiorentina T-bone veal steak

costata di manzo T-bone beef steak

cotechino spiced pork sausage for boiling

cotoletta veal, pork, or lamb chop

cotoletta ai ferri grilled veal or pork chop

cotoletta alla milanese veal chop in breadcrumbs

cotoletta alla valdostana
veal chop with ham and
cheese, in breadcrumbs

cotolette di agnello
lamb chops

cotolette di maiale pork
chops

cozze mussels

cozze alla marinara mussels
in white wine

crema custard dessert made
with eggs and milk

crema al caffè coffee
custard dessert

crema al cioccolato
chocolate custard dessert

crema di funghi cream of
mushroom soup

crema di piselli cream of
pea soup

crema pasticciera
confectioner's custard

crêpes Suzette pancakes
flambéed with orange
sauce

crescente fried bread made
with flour, lard, and eggs

crespelle savoury pancakes

crostata di frutta fruit tart

D, E

dadi bouillon cubes

datteri dates

degustazione di vini wine
tasting

dentice al forno baked
dentex (type of sea
bream)

digestivo digestive liqueur

Dolcelatte creamy blue
cheese

dolci sweets, desserts, cakes

endivia belga white chicory

entrecôte (di manzo) beef
entrecote

espresso strong, black coffee

F

fagiano pheasant

fagioli beans

fagioli borlotti in umido
borlotti borlotti beans in
tomatoes and vegetables

fagiolini long, green beans

faraona guinea fowl

farcito stuffed

fegato liver

fegato alla veneta liver in
butter with onions

fegato con salvia e burro
liver in butter and sage

fettuccine ribbon-shaped
pasta

fichi figs

filetti di pesce persico fillets
of perch

filetti di sogliola fillets
of sole

filetto ai ferri grilled fillet
of beef

filetto al cognac fillet of
beef flambé

filetto al pepe verde
fillet of beef with green
peppercorns

filetto al sangue rare fillet
of beef

filetto ben cotto well-done
fillet of beef

filetto (di manzo) fillet
of beef

filetto medio medium-
cooked fillet of beef

finocchi gratinati fennel
au gratin

finocchio fennel

fonduta cheese fondue

formaggi misti variety of
cheeses

fragole strawberries

fragole con gelato/panna
strawberries and ice
cream/cream

frappé fruit or milk shake
with crushed ice

Frascati dry white wine from
area around Rome

frittata type of omelette

frittata alle erbe herb
omelette

fritto deep fried
fritto misto mixed seafood in batter
frittura di pesce variety of fried fish
frutta fruit
frutta alla fiamma fruit flambé
frutta secca dried nuts and raisins
frutti di bosco mixture of strawberries, raspberries, mulberries, etc
frutti di mare seafood
funghi mushrooms
funghi trifolati mushrooms fried in garlic and parsley

G

gamberetti shrimps
gamberi prawns
gamberoni king prawns
gazzosa clear lemonade
gelatina jelly
gelato ice cream
gelato di crema vanilla-flavoured ice cream
gelato di frutta fruit-flavoured ice cream
gnocchetti verdi agli spinaci e al gorgonzola small flour, potato, and spinach dumplings with melted gorgonzola
gnocchi small flour and potato dumplings
gnocchi alla romana small milk and semolina dumplings with butter
Gorgonzola strong blue cheese from Lombardy
grancevola spiny spider crab
granchio crab
granita sorbet made of sweetened syrup
grigliata di pesce grilled fish
grigliata mista mixed grill (meat or fish)
grissini thin, crisp breadsticks
Gruviera Gruyère cheese

I

indivia endive
insalata salad
insalata caprese salad of tomatoes and mozzarella
insalata di funghi porcini boletus mushroom salad
insalata di mare seafood salad
insalata di nervetti boiled beef or veal tendons served cold with beans and pickles
insalata di pomodori tomato salad
insalata di riso rice salad
insalata mista mixed salad
insalata russa Russian salad
insalata verde green salad
involtini meat rolls stuffed with ham and herbs

L

lamponi raspberries
lasagne al forno layers of pasta baked in meat sauce with cheese
latte milk
latte macchiato con cioccolato hot milk sprinkled with cocoa
lattuga lettuce
leggero light
legumi legumes or pulses
lemonsoda sparkling lemon drink
lenticchie lentils
lepre hare
limonata lemon-flavoured fizzy drink
limone lemon
lingua tongue

M

macedonia di frutta fruit salad
maiale pork
maionese mayonnaise
mandarino mandarin
mandorla almond

manzo beef

marroni large chestnuts

Marsala fortified wine

marzapane marzipan

Mascarpone soft, mild cheese

medaglioni di vitello veal medallions

mela apple

melagrana pomegranate

melanzane aubergine

melone melon

menta mint

meringata meringue pie

merluzzo cod

merluzzo alla pizzaiola cod in tomato sauce with anchovies and capers

merluzzo in bianco cod with oil and lemon

messicani in gelatina rolls of veal in jelly

millefoglie pastry layered with custard

minestra in brodo noodle soup

minestrone vegetable soup with rice or pasta

mirtilli bilberries

more mulberries or blackberries

moscato sweet wine

mousse al cioccolato chocolate mousse

Mozzarella soft cheese

mozzarella in carrozza fried slices of bread and mozzarella

N, O

nasello hake

nocciole hazelnuts

noce moscata nutmeg

noci walnuts

nodino veal chop

olio oil

origano oregano

ossobuco stewed shin of veal

ostriche oysters

P

paglia e fieno mixed plain and green tagliatelle

paillard di manzo slices of grilled beef

paillard di vitello slices of grilled veal

pane bread

panino filled roll; bread roll

panna cream

parmigiana di melanzane aubergines baked with cheese

pasta al forno pasta baked in white sauce and grated cheese

pasta e fagioli thick soup with borlotti beans and pasta rings

pasta e piselli pasta with peas

pasticcio di fegato d'oca baked pasta dish with goose liver

pasticcio di lepre baked pasta dish with hare

pasticcio di maccheroni baked macaroni

pastina in brodo soup with small pasta

patate potatoes

patate al forno/arrosto roast potatoes

patate fritte chips

patate in insalata potato salad

Pecorino strong, hard cheese made from sheep's milk

penne pasta quills

penne ai quattro formaggi pasta with four cheeses sauce

penne all'arrabbiata pasta with tomato and chilli pepper sauce

penne panna e prosciutto pasta with cream and ham sauce

pepe pepper (spice)

peperoncino crushed chilli pepper

peperoni peppers

peperoni ripieni stuffed peppers

peperoni sott'olio peppers in oil

pera pear

pesca peach

pesce fish

pesce al cartoccio fish baked in foil with herbs

pesce in carpione marinaded fish

pesto sauce of basil, pine nuts, Parmesan, garlic, and oil

Pinot dry white wine from the Veneto region

pinzimonio sauce with oil and vinegar served with raw vegetables

piselli peas

piselli al prosciutto peas with ham and basil

pizzaiola slices of cooked beef in tomato sauce, oregano, and anchovies

pizzoccheri alla Valtellinese pasta strips with vegetables and cheese

polenta boiled cornmeal left to set and sliced

polenta e osei polenta with small birds

polenta pasticciata layers of polenta, tomato sauce, and cheese

pollo chicken

pollo alla cacciatora chicken in white wine with onions and carrots

pollo alla diavola deep-fried chicken pieces

polpette meatballs

polpettone meatloaf

pomodori tomatoes

pomodori ripieni stuffed tomatoes

pompelmo grapefruit

porri leeks

prezzemolo parsley

primi piatti first courses

prosciutto cotto cooked ham

prosciutto crudo type of cured ham

prugne plums

punte di asparagi all'agro asparagus tips in oil and lemon

purè di patate mashed potatoes

puttanesca tomato sauce with anchovies, capers, and black olives

Q, R

quaglie quails

radicchio red chicory

ragù meat-based sauce

rapanelli radishes

ravioli stuffed pasta parcels

ravioli al pomodoro meat ravioli in tomato sauce

razza skate

Ricotta type of cottage cheese

risi e bisi risotto with peas and ham

riso rice

risotto rice cooked in stock

risotto alla castellana risotto with mushroom, ham, cream, and cheese

risotto alla milanese risotto with saffron

risotto al nero di seppia risotto with cuttlefish ink

risotto al tartufo truffle risotto

roast-beef all'inglese thinly sliced cold roast beef

Robiola type of soft cheese from Lombardy

rognone trifolato kidney in garlic, oil, and parsley

rosatello/rosato rosé wine

rosmarino rosemary

S

salame salami

sale salt

salmone affumicato smoked salmon

salsa cocktail/rosa mayonnaise and ketchup sauce for fish and seafood

salsa di pomodoro tomato sauce

salsa tartara tartar sauce

salsa vellutata white sauce made with clear broth

salsa verde sauce for meat, with parsley and oil

salsiccia sausage

salsiccia di cinghiale wild boar sausage

salsiccia di maiale pork sausage

saltimbocca alla romana slices of veal stuffed with ham and sage and fried

salvia sage

sambuca (con la mosca) aniseed-flavour liqueur served with a coffee bean

sarde ai ferri grilled sardines

scaloppine veal escalopes

scaloppine al prezzemolo veal escalopes with parsley

scamorza alla griglia grilled soft cheese

scampi alla griglia grilled scampi

secco dry

secondi piatti second courses, main courses

sedano celery

selvaggina game

semifreddo cake or dessert often containing cream and served chilled

senape mustard

seppie in umido stewed cuttlefish

servizio compreso service charge included

servizio escluso service charge excluded

Soave dry white wine from the Veneto region

sogliola sole

sogliola ai ferri grilled sole

sogliola al burro sole cooked in butter

sogliola alla mugnaia sole cooked in flour and butter

sorbetto sorbet, soft ice cream

soufflé al formaggio cheese soufflé

soufflé al prosciutto ham soufflé

speck cured, smoked ham

spezzatino di vitello veal stew

spiedini assorted chunks of spit-cooked meat or fish

spinaci spinach

spinaci all'agro spinach with oil and lemon

spremuta di... freshly squeezed...juice

spumante sparkling wine

Stracchino soft cheese from Lombardy

stracciatella soup of beaten eggs in clear broth

strudel di mele apple strudel

stufato braised

succo di... ...juice

sugo al tonno tomato sauce with tuna, garlic, and parsley

T

tacchino ripieno stuffed turkey

tagliata finely cut beef fillet cooked in the oven

tagliatelle thin ribbon-shaped pasta

tagliatelle rosse tagliatelle made with beetroot

tagliatelle verdi tagliatelle made with spinach

tagliolini thin soup noodles

tartine small sandwiches

tartufo ice cream covered in cocoa or chocolate; truffle

tè tea

tiramisù dessert with coffee-soaked sponge, Marsala, Mascarpone, and cocoa powder

tonno tuna

torta tart, flan

torta di ricotta type of cheesecake

torta salata savoury flan

tortellini pasta shapes filled with minced pork, ham, Parmesan, and nutmeg

trancio di palombo smooth dogfish steak

trancio di pesce spada swordfish steak

trenette col pesto flat spaghetti with pesto sauce

triglia mullet (fish)

trippa tripe

trota trout

trota affumicata smoked trout

trota al burro trout cooked in butter

trota alle mandorle trout with almonds

trota bollita boiled trout

U

uccelletti small birds wrapped in bacon, served on cocktail sticks

uova eggs

uova alla coque soft-boiled eggs

uova al tegamino con pancetta fried eggs and bacon

uova farcite eggs with tuna, capers, and mayonnaise filling

uova sode hard-boiled eggs

uva grapes

uva bianca white grapes

uva nera black grapes

V

vellutata di asparagi creamed asparagus with egg yolks

vellutata di piselli creamed peas with egg yolks

verdura vegetables

vermicelli long, very fine, thin pasta

vino wine

vino bianco white wine

vino da dessert dessert wine

vino da pasto table wine

vino da tavola table wine

vino rosso red wine

vitello veal

vitello tonnato cold sliced veal in tuna, anchovy, oil, and lemon sauce

vongole clams

W, Z

würstel hot dog

zabaglione creamy dessert of eggs, sugar, and Marsala

zafferano saffron

zucca pumpkin

zucchero sugar

zucchine courgettes

zucchine al pomodoro courgettes in tomato, garlic and parsley sauce

zucchine ripiene stuffed courgettes

zuccotto ice-cream cake with sponge fingers, cream, and chocolate

zuppa soup

zuppa di cipolle onion soup

zuppa di cozze mussel soup

zuppa di lenticchie lentil soup

zuppa di pesce fish soup

zuppa di verdura vegetable soup

zuppa inglese trifle

DICTIONARY ENGLISH–ITALIAN

The gender of an Italian noun is shown by the word for "the": **il** or **lo** (masculine), **la** (feminine), and their plural forms **i** or **gli** (masculine) and **le** (feminine). When **lo** or **la** are abbreviated to **l'** in front of a vowel or **h**, the gender of the noun is shown by the abbreviation **(m)** or **(f)** after it.

A

about **circa**
accident **l'incidente (m)**
accident and emergency
    il Pronto Soccorso
account number **il numero
    di conto**
adapter **l'adattatore (m)**
address **l'indirizzo (m)**
adult **l'adulto (m)**
aerobics **l'aerobica (f)**
aeroplane **l'aeroplano (m)**
after **dopo**
afternoon **il pomeriggio**
again **ancora**
air conditioning **l'aria
    condizionata (f)**
air stewardess **l'assistente
    di volo (f)**
airmail **la posta aerea**
airport **l'aeroporto (m)**
aisle seat **il posto vicino
    al corridoio**
all **tutto**
allergic **allergico/a**
almost **quasi**
alone **solo/a**
already **già**
ambulance **l'ambulanza (f)**
and **e**
ankle **la caviglia**
another **altro/a**
answering machine
    la segreteria telefonica
antibiotics **gli antibiotici**
anything **qualcosa**
anything **niente**
appointment
    l'appuntamento (m)
April **aprile**
apron **il grembiule**

arm **il braccio**
armband **il bracciolo**
arrive (verb) **arrivare**
arrivals hall **gli arrivi**
art gallery **la galleria d'arte**
arthritis **l'artrite (f)**
artificial sweetener
    il dolcificante
as **come**
asthma **l'asma (f)**
at **a**
audio guide **la guida
    audio**
August **agosto**
Australia **Australia (f)**
automatic ticket machine
    la biglietteria automatica
autumn **l'autunno (m)**
awful **orribile**

B

babysitting **il servizio
    di babysitting**
back (body) **la schiena**
back (not front of) **la parte
    posteriore**
backpack **lo zaino**
bad **cattivo/a**
bag **la borsa**
baggage allowance
    il bagaglio consentito
baggage reclaim **il ritiro
    bagagli**
baker's **la panetteria**
baking tray **la teglia
    da forno**
balcony **il balcone**
ball **la palla**
ballet **la danza**
bandage **la benda**
bank **la banca**

bank account il conto bancario

bank holiday il giorno festivo

bank manager il direttore della banca

bar il bar

baseball mitt il guanto da baseball

basket il cestino

basketball la palla da baske

bath il bagno

bath robe l'accappatoio (m)

bathroom il bagno

battery la batteria

be (verb) essere

beach la spiaggia

beach ball il pallone da spiaggia

beach towel il telo da spiaggia

beautiful bello/a

bed il letto

bee l'ape (f)

before prima di

beginner principiante (m/f)

behind dietro a

below sotto

belt la cintura

beneath sotto

beside vicino a

bicycle la bicicletta

big grande

bikini il bikini

bill il conto

black nero/a

blanket la coperta

blender il frullatore

blood pressure la pressione sanguigna

blood test le analisi del sangue

blue blu

board (verb) imbarcarsi

boarding gate l'uscita d'imbarco (f)

boarding pass la carta d'imbarco

boat la barca

body il corpo

body lotion la crema per il corpo

bonnet (car) il cofano

book il libro

book shop la libreria

book (verb) prenotare

boot (car) il bagagliaio

boot lo stivale

bottle la bottiglia

bottle opener l'apribottiglie (m)

boutique la boutique

bowl la scodella

box la scatola

boy il ragazzo

boyfriend il fidanzato

bracelet il bracciale

breakdown il guasto

breakfast la colazione

briefcase la valigetta

British britannico/a

broken rotto/a

bruise l'ematoma (m)

brush (cleaning) la scopa

bubblebath il bagnoschiuma

bucket lo secchi

bumper il paraurti

burgle (verb) svaligiare

burn la bruciatura

bus l'autobus (m)

bus station la stazione degli autobus

bus stop la fermata dell'autobus

business, on per lavoro

bust il busto

butcher's la macelleria

buy (verb) comprare

by da; vicino a

C

cabin la cabina

cable car la funivia

café il bar

calm calmo/a

camera la fotocamera

camera bag la borsa per fotocamera

camping kettle il bollitore

camping stove il fornetto da campeggio
campsite il campeggio
can (verb) potere
can (noun) la scatoletta
can opener l'apribottiglie (m)
Canada il Canada
canoe la canoa
capsule la capsula
car la macchina
car park il parcheggio
car rental desk l'ufficio dell'autonoleggio (m)
caravan il camper
carry (verb) portare
cash il denaro
cash (verb) riscuotere
cash machine il sportello bancomat
casino il casinò
casserole dish la casseruola
castle il castello
catamaran il catamarano
cathedral la cattedrale
CD il CD
central heating il riscaldamento centralizzato
centre il centro
chair lift la seggiovia
change (verb) cambiare
changing room il spogliatoio
channel (TV) il canale
charge (verb) addebitare
check in il check-in
check out (hotel) lasciare
check-out (supermarket) la cassa
cheek la guancia
cheers! cin cin!
cheque l'assegno (m)
cheque card la carta assegni
chequebook il libretto degli assegni
chest il torace
chewing gum la gomma da masticare
child bambino/a (m/f)
chin il mento

church la chiesa
cigarette la sigaretta
cinema il cinema
city la città
clean pulito/a
close (near) vicino
close (verb) chiudere
closed chiuso/a
clothes gli abiti
cloudy nuvoloso/a
clubbing andare in discoteca
coast la costa
coat il cappotto
coat hanger l'appendiabiti (m)
colander il colino
cold (illness) il raffreddore
cold freddo/a
colouring pencil la matita colorata
come (verb) venire
comic il fumetto
compartment il scompartimento
compass la bussola
complain (verb) reclamare
computer il computer
concert il concerto
concourse l'atrio (m)
conditioner il balsamo
constipation la stitichezza
consul il console
consulate il consolato
contact number il numero di telefono
contents il contenuto
coolbox il frigo portatile
corkscrew il cavatappi
cot il lettino
couchette la cuccetta
cough la tosse
country il paese
courier il corriere
course il piatto
cream (lotion) la crema
credit card la carta di credito
crime il reato
cross trainer l'ellittica (f)

cufflinks gli gemelli
cup la tazza
cut il taglio
cutlery le posate
cycling helmet il casco

D

damaged danneggiato/a
dancing ballare
dashboard il cruscotto
daughter la figlia
day il giorno
December dicembre
deck chair la sedia a sdraio
degrees gradi
delayed ritardo
delicatessen la gastronomia
delicious delizioso/a
dentist la dentista
deodorant il deodorante
departure board il tabellone
  delle partenze
departures hall le partenze
deposit il deposito
desk la scrivania
detergent il detergente
develop (film) sviluppare
diabetic diabetico/a
diarrhoea la diarrea
diesel il diesel
digital camera la fotocamera
  digitale
dining car la carrozza
  ristorante
dinner la cena
disabled parking
  il parcheggio per disabili
dish il piatto
divorced divorziato/a
do (verb) fare
doctor il dottore
doctor's surgery
  l'ambulatorio (m)
dog il cane
doll la bambola
door la porta
double bed il letto
  matrimoniale
double room la camera
  doppia

drawing il disegno
dress l'abito (m)
dressing la fasciatura
drink (verb) bere
drink (noun) la bibita
drive (verb) guidare
driving licence la patente
  di guida
dry (wine) secco
dry (day; clothes) asciutto
during durante
dust pan la paletta
dustbin la pattumiera
duty-free shop il negozio
  duty-free
DVD player il lettore DVD

E

each (every) ogni
each ciascuno
early presto
ear l'orecchio (m)
east l'est (m)
eat (verb) mangiare
eight otto
elbow il gomito
electric razor il rasoio
  elettrico
electrician l'elettricista (m)
electricity l'elettricità (f)
eleven undici
email l'e-mail (f)
email address l'indirizzo
  e-mail (m)
embassy l'ambasciata (f)
emergency services
  gli servizi di emergenza
empty vuoto/a
engine il motore
English inglese
engraving l'incisione (f)
enjoy (verb) divertirsi
entrance l'entrata (f)
entrance ticket il biglietto
  d'entrata
envelope la busta
epileptic epilettico/a
equipment l'attrezzatura (f)
euro l'euro (m)
evening la sera

evening dress l'abito
da sera (m)
examine (verb) esaminare
exchange rate il tasso
di cambio
excursion l'escursione (f)
exercise bike la bicicletta
exhaust (car) la marmitta
exit l'uscita (f)
expensive caro/a
express service il servizio
espresso
extension lead la prolunga
extra extra
eye l'occhio (m)

F

face il viso
fairground il luna park
family la famiglia
family room la camera
familiare
family ticket il biglietto
famiglia
fan il ventilatore
far lontano
fare la tariffa
fast veloce
father il padre
favourite preferito/a
February febbraio
ferry il traghetto
fifty cinquanta
film (camera) il rullino
find (verb) trovare
fine (legal) la multa
finger il dito
finish (verb) finire
fire alarm l'allarme
antincendio (m)
fire engine l'autopompa (f)
fire extinguisher l'estintore
(m)
firefighter il pompiere
first primo/a
fish il pesce
fishmonger il pescivendolo
five cinque
fix (verb) riparare
flash gun il flash

flash photography
la fotografia con il flash
flight il volo
flight meal il pasto a bordo
flip-flop l'infradito (m)
flippers le pinne
float la tavoletta
flu l'influenza (f)
food il cibo
foot il piede
football (ball) il pallone
football (game) il calcio
for per
fork la forchetta
forty quaranta
four quattro
fracture la frattura
free (not occupied) libero/a
free (no charge) gratis
fresh fresco/a
Friday venerdì
fridge-freezer il frigorifero
congelatore
friend l'amico/a (m/f)
from da
front; in front of davanti;
di fronte a
frying pan la padella
fuel gauge l'indicatore di
livello del carburante (m)
full pieno/a
furniture shop il negozio
di arredamento
fuse box la scatola
dei fusibili

G

gallery (theatre) la galleria
game il gioco
garage il garage
garden il giardino
garlic l'aglio (m)
gas il gas
gate il cancello
gear stick la leva del cambio
get off (verb) scendere
gift il regalo
gift shop il negozio di
articoli da regalo
girl la ragazza

girlfriend la fidanzata

give (verb) dare

glass il vetro

glass (drinking) il bicchiere

glasses gli occhiali

gloss lucido

go (verb) andare

go out (verb) uscire

goggles gli occhialini

golf il golf

golf ball la palla da golf

golf club la mazza

golf course il campo da golf

golf tee il tee

good buono/a

goodbye arrivederci

good evening buonasera

good night buonanotte

grater la grattugia

graze l'escoriazione (f)

Great Britain la Gran Bretagna

green verde

greengrocer il fruttivendolo

grill pan la griglia

group il gruppo

guarantee la garanzia

guest l'ospite (m/f)

guide (person) la guida

guidebook la guida

guided tour la visita guidata

gym la palestra

H

hair i capelli

hairdryer l'asciugacapelli (m)

half la metà; mezzo/a (adj)

hand la mano

hand luggage il bagaglio a mano

handbag la borsa

handle la maniglia

happen (verb) succedere

happy contento/a; felice

harbour il porto

hardware shop la ferramenta

hatchback il portellone

hate (verb) odiare

have (verb) avere

hayfever il raffreddore da fieno

hazard lights le frecce lampeggianti

he egli; lui

head la testa

headache il mal di testa

head rest il poggiatesta

headlight i fari

health la salute

health insurance l'assicurazione sanitaria

hear (verb) sentire

heart condition la patologia cardiaca

heater l'impianto di riscaldamento (m)

heating il riscaldamento

heel il tallone

hello ciao; buongiorno

hello (on phone) pronto

help (verb) aiutare

her (object) lei

her (possessive) suo/sua (sing)/sue/suoi (plural)

here qui

high blood pressure la pressione arteriosa elevata

high chair il seggiolone

high-speed train il treno ad alta velocità

hiking l'escursionismo (m)

him lui

hire (verb) noleggiare

hold (verb) tenere

holdall la sacca da viaggio

holiday la vacanza

horn il clacson

horse riding andare a cavallo

hospital l'ospedale (m)

hot caldo/a

hotel l'albergo (m)

hour l'ora (f)

house la casa

hovercraft il hovercraft

how much? quanto?

how come?

how many? **quanti/e?**
humid **umido/a**
hundred **cento**
hurry (verb) **affrettarsi**
husband **il marito**
hydrofoil **l'aliscafo** (m)
hydrant **l'idrante** (m)

I

I (1st person) **io**
ice **il ghiaccio**
icy **ghiacciato/a**
ID **la carta d'identità**
ill **malato/a**
illness **la malattia**
in **in**
inhaler **l'inalatore** (m)
injection **l'iniezione** (f)
injure (verb) **ferirsi**
insect repellent **il repellente
per gli insetti**
insurance **l'assicurazione** (f)
insurance company **l'agenzia
assicurativa** (f)
insurance policy **la polizza
assicurativa**
intensive care unit **il reparto
di terapia intensiva**
interest (verb) **interessare**
interesting **interessante**
internet **l'Internet** (m)
internet café **il Internet cafè**
interpreter **l'interprete** (m/f)
inventory **l'inventario** (m)
iPod **l'iPod** (m)
iron **il ferro da stiro**
ironing board **l'asse
a stiro** (f)
it **esso/a; lo/la/l'; gli/le**
Italian **italiano/a**
Italy **l'Italia** (f)

J

jacket **la giacca**
January **gennaio**
jaw **la mascella**
jazz club **il jazz club**
jeans **i jeans**
jellyfish **la medusa**
jet ski **il moto d'acqua**

jeweller **il gioielliere**
jewellery **la gioielleria**
July **luglio**
jumper **il maglione**
June **giugno**

K

keep straight **andare dritto**
kettle **il bollitore**
key **la chiave**
keyboard **la tastiera**
kilo **il chilo**
kilometre **il chilometro**
kitchen **la cucina**
knee **il ginocchio**
knife **il coltello**
knock down (verb) **colpire**
know (people) **conoscere**
know (a fact) **sapere**

L

lake **il lago**
laptop **il computer portatile**
large **grande**
last **ultimo/a**
late **tardi; in ritardo**
lawyer **l'avvocato** (m)
leak **la perdita**
leave (verb) **lasciare; partire**
left **sinistra**
left luggage **il deposito
bagagli**
leisure activities **le attività
del tempo libero**
leg **la gamba**
lens **la lente**
lifebuoy **il salvagente**
lifeguard **il bagnino**
life jacket **il giubbotto
di salvataggio**
lift **l'ascensore** (m)
lift pass **il pass per lo ski-lift**
light **leggero/a**
light (noun) **la luce**
light (verb) **accendere**
light bulb **la lampadina**
lighter **l'accendino** (m)
lighthouse **il faro**
like (verb) **piacere**
line **la linea**

list **la lista**
listen (verb) **ascoltare**
little **poco; piccolo**
local **locale**
lock **il lucchetto**
lock (verb) **chiudere a chiave**
log on (verb) **connettersi**
log out (verb) **disconnettersi**
long **lungo**
look (verb) **guardare**
lose (verb) **perdere**
lost property **l'ufficio oggetti smarriti** (m)
love (verb) **amare**
luggage **il bagaglio**
lunch **il pranzo**

M

magazine **la rivista**
make (verb) **fare**
mallet **il maglio**
man **l'uomo** (m)
manual **il manuale**
manuscript **il manoscritto**
many **molti/e**
map **la mappa; la cartina**
marina **il porticciolo**
market **il mercato**
married **sposato/a**
match (sport) **la partita**
match (light) **il fiammifero**
matt **opaco/a**
mattress **il materasso**
May **maggio**
mechanic **il meccanico**
medicine **la medicina**
medium **mezzo**
memory card **la scheda di memoria**
memory stick **la chiavetta USB**
mend (verb) **riparare**
menu **il menù**
message **il messaggio**
microwave **il forno a microonde**
midday **mezzogiorno**
middle **mezzo**
midnight **mezzanotte**

mini bar **il mini bar**
minute **il minuto**
mistake **l'errore** (m)
misty **nebbioso/a**
mixed **misto/a**
mixing bowl **l'insalatiera** (f)
mobile phone **il cellulare**
mole (medical) **il neo**
Monday **lunedì**
money **il denaro; i soldi**
month **il mese**
monument **il monumento**
mooring **l'ormeggio** (m)
more **più**
morning **il mattino**
mother **la madre**
motorbike **la motocicletta**
motorway **l'autostrada** (f)
mountain **la montagna**
mountain bike **la mountain bike**
mouse (computer) **il mouse**
mouth **la bocca**
mouthwash **il collutorio**
much **molto**
museum **il museo**
music **la musica**
musician **il musicista**
must (verb) **dovere**
my **mio/mia/mie/miei**
myself **mi; me stesso/a**

N

nail **l'unghia** (f)
nail clippers **i tagliaunghie**
nail scissors **le forbicine per le unghie**
name **il nome**
napkin **il tovagliolo**
nausea **la nausea**
neck **il collo**
necklace **la collana**
need (verb) **aver bisogno**
newsagent **l'edicola** (f)
newspaper **il giornale**
never **mai**
next **prossimo/a**
next to **vicino a**
new **nuovo/a**
nice **bello/a; piacevole**

night la notte
nightclub il nightclub
nine nove
no no
north il nord
nose nil naso
nosebleed il sangue dal naso
not non
November novembre
number il numero
number plate il numero di targa
nurse l'infermiera (f)
nursery slopes le discese per i principianti

O

October ottobre
of di
off spento/a
often spesso
oil l'olio (m)
ointment la pomata
on (light) acceso/a
on su
one uno/a
online online
only solamente
open aperto/a
open (verb) aprire
opening hours l'orario di apertura (m)
opera l'opera (f)
opera house il teatro dell'opera
operation l'intervento chirurgico (m)
opposite davanti; di fronte
or o
orange (colour) arancione
order l'ordine (m)
order (verb) ordinare
other altro/a
our nostro/nostri/nostra/ nostre
outside fuori
oven il forno
oven gloves i guanti da forno

over su; sopra
overnight tutta la notte
owe (verb) essere in debito

P

pack (verb) fare le valigie
packet il pacchetto
pain il dolore
painkiller l'antidolorifico (m)
painting il dipinto
pair la coppia
paper la carta
papers (ID) i documenti
park il parco
park (verb) parcheggiare
parking il parcheggio
parking meter il parchimetro
passenger il passeggero
passport il passaporto
passport control il controllo passaporti
pay (verb) pagare
pay in (verb) effettuare un deposito
pedestrian crossing l'attraversamento pedonale (m)
peeler lo sbucciatore
pen la penna
pencil la matita
people la gente; le persone
perhaps forse
personal CD player il lettore CD
pet l'animale domestico (m)
petrol il carburante
petrol station la stazione di servizio
pharmacist il farmacista
pharmacy la farmacia
phone il telefono
phone call la telefonata
phone card la carta telefonica
photo album l'album delle fotografie (m)
photo frame la cornice
photograph la fotografia
photography la fotografia

pianist il pianista
picnic il picnic
picnic hamper il cestino da picnic
piece il pezzo
pilates pilates
pill la compressa
pillow il cuscino
pilot il pilota
PIN il PIN
pink rosa
place il luogo
plaster il cerotto
plate il piatto
platform il binario
play (games) (verb) giocare
playground l'area giochi (f)
please per favore
plug la spina
poles (ski) le racchette da sci
police la polizia
police car la volante
police station il commissariato
policeman il poliziotto
policewoman la poliziotta
policy la polizza
pool la piscina
porter il facchino
possible possibile
post la posta
post (verb) spedire la posta
post office l'ufficio postale (m)
postbox la cassetta delle lettere
postcard la cartolina
postman il postino
prefer (verb) preferire
pregnant incinta
prescription la ricetta medica
present il regalo
price il prezzo
print (verb) stampare
print (photo) la stampa
programme il programma
public holiday il giorno festivo

pump (bicycle) la pompa
puncture la gomma a terra
purse il portamonete
put (verb) mettere

Q, R

quarter il quarto
quick rapido/a; veloce
quite abbastanza
radiator il radiatore
radio la radio
railway la ferrovia
raining piovendo
rape la violenza carnale
rash l'eruzione (f)
razor il rasoio
read (verb) leggere
ready pronto/a
really veramente
receipt la ricevuta
reclaim tag la ricevuta dei bagagli
recommend (verb) consigliare
record shop il negozio di dischi
red rosso/a
reduction la riduzione
remote control il telecomando
rent (verb) affittare; noleggiare
repair (verb) riparare
report (noun) la denuncia
report (verb) denunciare
reservation la prenotazione
reserve (verb) prenotare; riservare
restaurant il ristorante
restaurant car la carrozza ristorante
resuscitation la rianimazione
retired in pensione
return ticket il biglietto di andata e ritorno
reverse charge call la chiamata a carico del destinatario
rides le giostre
right (direction) destra

river il fiume
road la strada
road signs segnali stradali (m pl)
rob (verb) derubare
robbery il furto
roll (film) il rullino
roofrack il bagagliaio
room la stanza; la camera
round rotondo/a
roundabout la rotatoria
rowing machine il vogatore
rubbish bin la pattumiera

S

safari park il parco safari
safe sicuro/a
sailing la vela
sailing boat la barca a vela
saloon car la berlina
same stesso/a
sand la sabbia
sandals i sandali
satellite TV la TV satellitare
Saturday sabato
saucepan la pentola
saucer il piattino
say (verb) dire
scan l'ecografia (f)
scissors le forbici
sea il mare
season la stagione
seat il posto; la sedia
second secondo/a
see (verb) vedere
sell (verb) vendere
sell-by date la data di scadenza
send (verb) inviare; mandare; spedire
senior citizen anziano/a
separately separatamente
September settembre
serious grave; serio/a
serve (verb) servire
seven sette
shampoo lo shampoo
shaving foam la schiuma da barba
she ella; lei

shirt la camicia
shoe la scarpa
shop il negozio
shopping fare la spesa
shopping mall il centro commerciale
shorts i calzoncini
shoulder la spalla
shower la doccia
shower gel il docciaschiuma
side effect l'effetto indesiderato (m)
side plate il piattino
signpost il cartello
singer cantante (m/f)
single room la camera singola
single ticket il biglietto di sola andata
six sei
size la taglia
ski boots gli scarponi da sci
skiing lo sci
skin la pelle
skis gli sci
skirt la gonna
sleeping bag lo sacco a pelo
slice la fetta
sliproad la bretella
slow lento/a
small piccolo/a
smoke (verb) fumare
smoke alarm il rivelatore di fumo
snack lo spuntino
snake il serpente
sneeze (verb) starnutire
snorkel il boccaglio
snow (verb) nevicare
snowboard lo snowboard
so così
soap il sapone
socks i calzini
soft toy il peluche
some alcuni/e
somebody qualcuno/a
something qualcosa
sometimes qualche volta
soon presto
sore infiammato/a

sorry scusi
south il sud
souvenir il souvenir
spare tyre la ruota di scorta
spatula la spatola
speak (verb) parlare
speciality la specialità
speed limit il limite
di velocità
speedometer il tachimetro
splint la stecca
splinter la scheggia
spoon il cucchiaio
sport lo sport
sports centre il centro
sportivo
sprain la distorsione
spray lo spray
spring la primavera
square (in town) la piazza
squash (game) lo squash
stairs le scale
stamp il francobollo
start (verb) cominciare
station la stazione
statue la statua
stay il soggiorno
step machine la step
machine
adhesive tape lo scotch
stolen rubato/a
stomach lo stomaco
stomach ache il mal di
stomaco
stop (bus) la fermata
stop (verb) fermare
stopcock il rubinetto di
arresto
stormy tempestoso/a
street la strada; la via
street map la cartina;
la mappa
string la corda
strong forte
student studente/
studentessa (m/f)
student card la carta
studenti
suit il completo
suitcase la valigia

summer l'estate (f)
sun il sole
sunburn la bruciatura
sunglasses gli occhiali
da sole
sunhat il cappello da sole
suntan lotion la lozione
solare
sun lounger il lettino sdraio
Sunday domenica
sunny assolato/a
sunscreen il filtro solare
supermarket il
supermercato
suppositories le supposte
surf (verb) fare surf
surfboard la tavola da surf
swimming il nuoto
swimming pool la piscina
swimsuit il costume

T

table il tavolo
tablet la compressa
tailor il sarto
take (verb) prendere
takeaway da portar via
taxi il taxi
taxi rank il posteggio
dei taxi
teaspoon il cucchiaino
teeth i denti
telephone il telefono
telephone (verb) telefonare
telephone box la cabina
del telefono
television (set) il televisore
tell (verb) dire
temperature la temperatura
ten dieci
tennis il tennis
tennis ball la palla da tennis
tennis court il campo
da tennis
tennis racquet la racchetta
da tennis
tent la tenda
tent peg il picchetto
terminal il terminal
than di

less meno
thank you grazie
that quello/a
the il/lo/la/i/gli/le
theatre il teatro
their loro
then poi; allora
there is/are c'è/ci sono
thermostat termostato (m)
thief ladro (m)
think (verb) pensare
this questo/a
thirty trenta
thousand mille
three tre
throat la gola
through attraverso
thumb il pollice
Thursday giovedì
ticket il biglietto
tight stretto
time il tempo
opening times l'orario di apertura (m)
timetable l'orario (m)
tobacco il tabacco
tobacconist il tabaccaio (m)
today oggi
toe il dito del piede
toilet il bagno
toll il pedaggio
tomorrow domani
tonight stasera
too (excessively) troppo
toothache il mal di denti
toothbrush lo spazzolino da denti
toothpaste il dentifricio
torch la torcia
tour il giro
tour guide la guida turistica
tourist turista (m/f)
tourist information office l'ufficio del turismo (m)
tow (verb) rimorchiare
towel l'asciugamano (m)
town la città
town centre il centro della città
town hall il municipio

toy il giocattolo
traffic jam l'ingorgo
traffic lights il semaforo
train il treno
trainers le scarpe da ginnastica
traveller's cheque il travellers cheque
trip la gita
trolley il carrello
try (verb) provare
t-shirt la t-shirt
Tuesday martedì
turn (verb) girare; voltare
turn off (verb) spegnere
twenty venti
twin bedded room la camera a due letti
two due
tyre il pneumatico
tyre pressure la pressione degli pneumatici

U

umbrella l'ombrello (m)
underground railway la metropolitana
understand (verb) capire: comprendere
United States gli Stati Uniti
unleaded senza piombo
until fino a
up su
urgent urgente
us noi
use (verb) usare
useful utile
usual solito/a
usually generalmente

V

vacancy (room) la stanza libera
vacuum flask il thermos
validate (verb) vidimare
valuables gli oggetti di valore
vegetarian vegetariano/a
venetian blind la tenda veneziana

very **molto**
video game **il videogioco**
view **la vista**
village **il villaggio**
vineyard **il vigneto**
visa **il visto**
visiting hours **l'orario delle visite**
visitor **il visitatore**

W

wait (verb) **aspettare**
waiting room **la sala d'attesa**
waiter **il cameriere**
waitress **la cameriera**
wake-up call **la sveglia telefonica**
walk **la passeggiata**
walking boots **gli scarponi**
wallet **il portafoglio**
want (verb) **volere**
ward **la corsia**
warm **caldo/a**
washing machine **la lavatrice**
wasp **la vespa**
watch (verb) **guardare**
water **l'acqua (f)**
waterfall **la cascata**
waterproofs **gli indumenti impermeabili**
water-skiing **lo sci d'acqua**
we **noi**
weather **il tempo**
website **il sito Web**
Wednesday **mercoledì**
week **la settimana**
weekend **il fine settimana**
welcome **benvenuto**
well **bene**
west **l'ovest (m)**
wet **bagnato/a**
what? **cosa?**
wheel **la ruota**
wheelchair **la sedia a rotelle**
wheelchair access **l'accesso per i disabili (m)**
wheelchair ramp **la rampa per i disabili**
when? **quando?**
where? **dove?**

which? **quale?**
whisk **rusta (f)**
white **bianco/a**
who? **chi?**
why? **perché?**
widescreen TV **il televisore a schermo panoramico**
wife **la moglie**
wind **il vento**
window **la finestra**
window seat **il posto vicino al finestrino**
windscreen **la parabrezza**
windscreen wiper **il tergicristallo**
windsurfer **surfista (m/f)**
windy **ventoso/a**
wine **il vino**
winter **l'inverno (m)**
wiper blades **le spazzole del tergicristallo**
with **con**
withdraw (money) (verb) **prelevare**
withdrawal **il prelievo**
without **senza**
witness **testimone (m/f)**
woman **la donna**
work **il lavoro**
work (verb) **lavorare**
work (machine) **funzionare**
wrap (a gift) **incartare**
wrapping paper **la carta a regalo**
wrist **il polso**
wrist watch **l'orologio da polso**
wrong **sbagliato/a**

X, Y, Z

X-ray **la radiografia**
yacht **lo yacht**
year **l'anno (m)**
yellow **giallo/a**
yes **sì**
yesterday **ieri**
yoga **lo yoga**
you **Lei; tu (singular); voi (plural)**
zoo **lo zoo**

DICTIONARY ITALIAN–ENGLISH

The gender of Italian nouns is shown by the abbreviations (m) for masculine and (f) for feminine. Plural nouns are followed by the abbreviations (m pl) or (f pl). Adjectives vary according to the gender and number of the word they describe. Here the masculine singular form (usually "o") is shown, followed by the alternative feminine ending (usually "a").

A

a at
abbastanza quite
abiti (m pl) clothes
abito (m) dress
abito da sera (m) evening dress
accamparsi to camp
accappatoio (m) bath robe
accendere to light
accendino (m) lighter
acceso on (light)
accesso per i disabili (m) wheelchair access
acqua (f) water
adattatore (m) adapter
addebitare to charge
adulto (m) adult
aerobica (f) aerobics
aeroplano (m) aeroplane
aeroporto (m) airport
affittare to rent
affrettarsi to hurry
agenzia assicurativa (f) insurance company
agosto August
airbag (m) airbag
aiutare to help
albergo (m) hotel
album delle fotografie (m) photo album
alcuni/e some
aliscafo (m) hydrofoil
allarme antincendio (m) fire alarm
allergico/a allergic
allora then
altro/a other; **un altro/ un'altra** another
ambasciata (f) embassy

ambulanza (f) ambulance
ambulatorio (m) doctor's surgery
amico/a (m/f) friend
analisi del sangue (f pl) blood test
anche too (also)
ancora again
andare to go
andare a cavallo horse riding
andare in discoteca to go clubbing
andare dritto to go straight
animale (m) domestico (m) pet
anno (m) year
antibiotici (m pl) antibiotics
antidolorifico (m) painkiller
anziano/a (m/f) senior citizen
ape (f) bee
aperto/a open
appartamento (m) apartment
appendiabiti (m) coat hanger
appuntamento (m) appointment
apribottiglie (m) bottle/can opener
aprile April
aprire to open
arancione orange (colour)
area giochi (f) playground
aria condizionata (f) air conditioning
arrivare to arrive
arrivederci goodbye
arrivi (m pl) arrivals hall

arte (f) art
artrite (f) arthritis
ascensore (m) lift
asciugacapelli (m) hairdryer
asciugamano (m) towel
asciutto dry (day; clothes)
ascoltare to listen
asma (f) asthma
aspettare to wait
asse da stiro (f) ironing
board
assegno (m) cheque
assicurazione (f) insurance
assicurazione sanitaria (f)
health insurance
assistente di volo (f) air
stewardess
assolato/a sunny
atrio (m) concourse
attraversamento pedonale
(m) pedestrian crossing
attraverso through
attrezzatura (f) equipment
Australia (f) Australia
autobus (m) bus
automobile (f) car
autonoleggio (m) car rental
autopompa (f) fire engine
autostrada (f) motorway
autunno (m) autumn
aver bisogno to need
avere to have
avvocato (m) lawyer

B

bagagliaio (m) boot (car);
roofrack
bagaglio (m) luggage
bagaglio consentito (m)
baggage allowance
bagaglio a mano (m) hand
luggage
bagnato/a wet
bagnino (m) lifeguard
bagno (m) bath; bathroom;
toilet
bagnoschiuma (m)
bubblebath
balcone (m) balcony
ballare dancing

balsamo (m) conditioner
bambino/a (m/f) child
bambola (f) doll
banca (f) bank
bar (m) bar; café
barbecue (m) barbecue
barca (f) boat
barca a vela (f) sailing boat
baseball (m) baseball
batteria (f) battery
bello/a beautiful; nice
benda (f) bandage
bene alright; well
benvenuto welcome
bere to drink
berlina (f) saloon car
bianco/a white
bibita (f) drink (noun)
bicchiere (m) glass
(drinking)
bicicletta (f) bicycle;
exercise bike
bidet (m) bidet
biglietteria automatica (f)
automatic ticket machine
biglietto (m) ticket
biglietto di andata e ritorno
(m) return ticket
biglietto d'entrata (m)
entrance ticket
biglietto famiglia (m)
family ticket
biglietto di sola andata (m)
single ticket
bikini (m) bikini
binario (m) platform
blu blue
bocca (f) mouth
boccaglio (m) snorkel
bollitore (m) camping
kettle; kettle
bordo: a bordo on board
borsa (f) bag; handbag
borsa per fotocamera (f)
camera bag
bottiglia (f) bottle
boutique (f) boutique
bracciale (m) bracelet
braccio (m) arm
bretella (f) sliproad

britannico/a British
bruciatura (f) burn
buonanotte good night
buonasera good evening
buongiorno hello
buono/a good
bussola (f) compass
busta (f) envelope
busto (m) bust

C

c'è there is
cabina (f) cabin
cabina del telefono (f)
  telephone box
calcio (m) football (game)
caldo/a hot; warm
calmo/a calm
calzini (m pl) socks
calzoncini (m pl) shorts
cambiare to change
camera (f) room
camera a due letti (f) twin
  bedded room
camera doppia (f)
  double room
camera familiare (f)
  family room
camera singola (f)
  single room
cameriera (f) waitress
cameriere (m) waiter
camicia (f) shirt
camminare to walk
campeggio (m) campsite
camper (m) caravan
campo da golf (m)
  golf course
campo da tennis (m)
  tennis court
Canada (m) Canada
canale (m) channel (TV)
cancello (m) gate
cane (m) dog
canoa (f) canoe
cantante (m/f) singer
capelli (m pl) hair
capire to understand
cappello da sole (m)
  sunhat

cappotto (m) coat
capsula (f) capsule
carburante (m) petrol
caro/a expensive
carrello (m) trolley
carrozza ristorante (f)
  dining car
carta assegni (f)
  cheque card
carta di credito (f)
  credit card
carta d'identità (f) ID
carta d'imbarco (f)
  boarding pass
carta studenti (f)
  student card
carta telefonica (f)
  phone card
cartello (m) signpost
cartina (f) map; street map
cartolina (f) postcard
casa (f) house
cascata (f) waterfall
casco (m) cycling helmet
casinò (m) casino
cassa (f) check-out
  (supermarket)
casseruola (f) casserole dish
cassetta delle lettere (f)
  postbox
castello (m) castle
catamarano (m) catamaran
cattedrale (f) cathedral
cattivo/a bad
cavatappi (m) corkscrew
caviglia (f) ankle
cavolo (m) cabbage
CD (m) CD
cellulare (m) mobile phone
cena (f) dinner
cento hundred
centro commerciale (m)
  shopping mall
centro della città (m)
  town centre
centro sportivo (m)
  sports centre
cestino (m) basket
cestino da picnic (m)
  picnic hamper

check-in (m) check in
chi? who?
chiamata a carico del destinatario (f) reverse charge call
chiave (f) key
chiavetta USB (f) memory stick
chiesa (f) church
chilo (m) kilo
chilometro (m) kilometre
chiudere to close
chiudere a chiave to lock
chiuso/a closed
ci sono there are
ciao hello
ciascuno each
cibo (m) food
cin cin! cheers!
cinema (m) cinema
cinquanta fifty
cinque five
cintura (f) belt
circa about
città (f) city; town
clacson (m) horn
cofano (m) bonnet (car)
colazione (f) breakfast
colino (m) colander
collana (f) necklace
collo (m) neck
collutorio (m) mouthwash
colpire to knock down
coltello (m) knife
come as; how; like
come? how
commissariato (m) police station
completo (m) suit
comprare to buy
comprendere to understand
compressa (f) pill; tablet
computer (m) computer
computer portatile (m) laptop
con with
concerto (m) concert
connettersi to log on
conoscere to know (people)
consigliare to recommend

consolato (m) consulate
console (m) consul
contento/a happy
contenuto (m) contents
conto (m) bill
conto bancario (m) bank account
controllo passaporti (m) passport control
coperta (f) blanket
coppia (f) pair
corda (f) string
cornice (f) photo frame
corpo (m) body
corriere (m) courier
corsia (f) ward
cosa? what?
così so
costa (f) coast
costume (m) swimsuit
crema (f) cream
crema per il corpo (f) body lotion
cruscotto (m) dashboard
cuccetta (f) couchette
cucchiaino (m) teaspoon
cucchiaio (m) spoon
cucina (f) kitchen
cuscino (m) pillow

D

da by; from
danneggiato/a damaged
danza (f) ballet
dare to give
dare la precedenza to give way
data di scadenza (f) sell-by date
davanti front; in front of; opposite
delizioso/a delicious
denaro (m) cash; money
denti (m pl) teeth
dentifricio (m) toothpaste
dentista (m) dentist
denuncia (f) report (noun)
denunciare to report
deodorante (m) deodorant
depositare to deposit

deposito (m) deposit
deposito bagagli (m) left luggage
derubare to rob
destra: a destra right (direction)
detergente (m) detergent
detestare to hate
di of; than
diabetico/a diabetic
diarrea (f) diarrhoea
dicembre December
dieci ten
diesel diesel
dietro a behind
digitare to key
dipinto (m) painting
dire to say; to tell
direttore della banca (m) bank manager
disabile (m) disabled person
discese per i principianti (f pl) nursery slopes
disconnettersi to log out
disegno (m) drawing
distorsione (f) sprain
dito (m) finger
dito del piede (m) toe
divorziato/a divorced
doccia (f) shower
docciaschiuma (m) shower gel
documenti (m pl) papers (identity)
dodici twelve
dolce sweet; dessert
dolcificante (m) artificial sweetener
dolore (m) pain
domani tomorrow
domenica Sunday
donna (f) woman
dopo after
dottore (m) doctor
dove? where?
dovere to have to; must (verb)
due two
durante during

E

e and
ecografia (f) scan
edicola (f) newsagent
effetto indesiderato (m) side effect
effettuare un deposito to pay in
egli he
elettricista (m) electrician
elettricità (f) electricity
ella she
ellittica (f) cross trainer
e-mail (f) email
ematoma (m) bruise
entrata (f) entrance
epilettico/a epileptic
errore (m) mistake
eruzione (f) rash
esaminare to examine
escoriazione (f) graze
escursionismo (m) hiking
essere to be
essere in debito to owe
esso/a it
est (m) east
estate (f) summer
estintore (m) fire extinguisher
euro (m) euro
extra extra

F

facchino (m) porter
famiglia (f) family
fare to do; to make
fare la spesa to go shopping
fare le valigie to pack
fare surf to surf
fari (m pl) headlights
farmacia (f) pharmacy
farmacista (m) pharmacist
faro (m) lighthouse
fasciatura (f) dressing
febbraio February
felice happy
fermare to stop
fermata dell'autobus (f) bus stop

ferramenta (f)
   hardware shop
ferrovia (f) railway
fetta (f) slice
fiammifero (m) match
   (light)
fidanzata (f) girlfriend
fidanzato (m) boyfriend
figlia (f) daughter
filtro solare (m) sunscreen
fine settimana (m)
   weekend
finire to finish
fino a until
firmare to sign
fiume (m) river
flash (m) flash gun
forbici (f pl) scissors
forbicine per le unghie
   (f pl) nail scissors
forchetta (f) fork
fornetto da campeggio (m)
   camping stove
forno (m) oven
forno a microonde (m)
   microwave
forse perhaps
forte strong
fotocamera (f) camera
fotocamera digitale (f)
   digital camera
fotografia (f) photograph
fotografia con il flash (f)
   flash photography
francobollo (m) stamp
frattura (f) fracture
frecce lampeggianti (f pl)
   hazard lights
freddo/a cold
fresco/a fresh
frigo portatile (m) coolbox
frigorifero congelatore (m)
   fridge-freezer
fronte: di fronte a front; in
   front of; opposite
frullatore (m) blender
fruttivendolo (m)
   greengrocer
fumare to smoke
fumetto (m) comic

funivia (f) cable car
funzionare to work
   (machine)
fuori outside
furto (m) robbery

G

galleria (f) gallery (theatre)
galleria d'arte (f) art gallery
gamba (f) leg
garage (m) garage
garanzia (f) guarantee
gas (m) gas
gastronomia (f)
   delicatessen
gemelli (m pl) cufflinks
generalmente usually
gennaio January
gente (f) people
ghiacciato/a icy
ghiaccio (m) ice
già already
giacca (f) jacket
giallo/a yellow
giardino (m) garden
ginocchio (m) knee
giocare to play (games)
giocattolo (m) toy
gioco (m) game
gioielleria (f) jewellery
gioielliere (m) jeweller
giornale (m) newspaper
giorno (m) day
giorno festivo (m) bank
   holiday
giostre (f pl) rides
giovedì Thursday
giro (m) tour
gita (f) trip
giubbotto di salvataggio
   (m) life jacket
giugno June
giusto/a right (correct)
gli the (m pl)
gola (f) throat
golf (m) golf
gomito (m) elbow
gomma a terra (f) puncture
gomma da masticare (f)
   chewing gum

gonna (f) skirt
gradi degrees
Gran Bretagna (f) Great Britain
grande big; large
gratis free (no charge)
grattugia (f) grater
grave serious
grazie thank you
grembiule (m) apron
griglia (f) grill pan
gruppo (m) group
guancia (f) cheek
guanti da forno (m pl) oven gloves
guanto da baseball (m) baseball mitt
guardare to look; to watch
guasto (m) breakdown
guida (f) guide; guidebook
guida audio (f) audio guide
guida turistica (f) tour guide
guidare to drive

H, I, J

hovercraft (m) hovercraft
idrante (m) hydrant
i the (m pl)
ieri yesterday
il the (m)
imbarcarsi to board
imbarcazione da diporto (f) pleasure boat
impianto di riscaldamento (m) heater
impianto stereo dell' automobile (m) car stereo
in in
inalatore (m) inhaler
incartare to gift-wrap
incidente (m) accident
incinta pregnant
incisione (f) engraving
indicatore di livello del carburante (m) fuel gauge
indirizzo (m) address
indirizzo e-mail (m) email address
indumenti impermeabili (m pl) waterproofs

infermiera (f) nurse
infiammato/a sore
influenza (f) flu
infradito (m) flip-flop
inglese English
ingorgo (m) traffic jam
iniezione (f) injection
insalatiera (f) mixing bowl
interessante interesting
interessare to interest
Internet (m) internet
Internet cafè (m) internet café
interprete (m/f) interpreter
intervento chirurgico (m) operation (medical)
inventario (m) inventory
inverno (m) winter
inviare to send
io I
iPod (m) iPod
Italia (f) Italy
italiano/a Italian
jazz club (m) jazz club
jeans (m pl) jeans

L

la the (f)
là over there
ladro (m) thief
lago (m) lake
lampadina (f) light bulb
lasciare to check out (hotel); to leave; to vacate
lassù up there
lavatrice (f) washing machine
lavorare to work
lavoro (m) work; per lavoro on business
le the (f pl)
leggere to read
leggero/a light
lei her (object)
lei she; Lei you
lente (f) lens
lento/a slow
lettino (m) cot
lettino sdraio (m) sun lounger

letto (m) bed
letto matrimoniale (m) double bed
lettore CD (m) CD player
lettore DVD (m) DVD player
leva del cambio (f) gear stick
libero/a free (not occupied)
libreria (f) book shop
libretto degli assegni (m) chequebook
libro (m) book
limite di velocità (m) speed limit
linea (f) line
lista (f) list
lo the (m)
locale local
lontano far
loro their; they
lozione solare (f) suntan lotion
lucchetto (m) lock
luce (f) light (noun)
lucido gloss
luglio July
lui he; him
luna park (m) fairground
lunedì Monday
lungo/a long
luogo (m) place

M

macchina (f) car; machine
macelleria (f) butcher's
madre (f) mother
maggio May
maglio (m) mallet
maglione (m) jumper
mai never
mal di denti (m) toothache
mal di stomaco stomach ache
mal di testa (m) headache
malato/a ill
malattia (f) illness
mandare to send
mangiare to eat
maniglia (f) handle
mano (f) hand

manoscritto (m) manuscript
mappa (f) map; street map
mare (m) sea
marito (m) husband
marmitta (f) exhaust (car)
martedì Tuesday
mascella (f) jaw
materasso (m) mattress
matita (f) pencil
mattino (m) morning
mazza (f) golf club
meccanico (m) mechanic
medicina (f) medicine
medusa (f) jellyfish
meno less
mento (m) chin
menù (m) menu
mercato (m) market
mercoledì Wednesday
mese (m) month
messaggio (m) message
metà half
metropolitana (f) underground railway
mettere to put
mezzanotte midnight
mezzo medium; middle; half
mezzogiorno midday
mia/mie my (f/f pl)
mini bar (m) mini bar
minuto (m) minute
mio/miei my (m/m pl)
misto/a mixed
modulo (m) form
moglie (f) wife
molti/e many
moltissimo very much
molto much; very
montagna (f) mountain
monumento (m) monument
moto d'acqua (m) jet ski
motocicletta (f) motorbike
motore (m) engine
mountain bike (f) mountain bike
mouse (m) mouse (computer)
multa (f) fine (legal)
municipio (m) town hall

museo (m) museum
musica (f) music
musicista (m) musician

N

naso (m) nose
nausea (f) nausea
nebbioso/a misty
negozio (m) shop
negozio di arredamento
(m) furniture shop
negozio di articoli da
regalo (m) gift shop
negozio di dischi record
shop
negozio duty-free (m)
duty-free shop
neo (m) mole (medical)
nero/a black
niente anything; nothing
nightclub (m) nightclub
no no
noi us; we
noleggiare to hire; to rent
nome (m) name
non not
nord (m) north
nostro/nostri/nostra/
nostre our
notte (f) night
nove nine
novembre November
numero (m) number
numero di conto (m)
account number
numero di targa (m)
registration number
numero di telefono (m)
contact number
nuoto (m) swimming
nuovo/a new
nuvoloso/a cloudy

O

o or
occhiali (m pl) glasses
occhiali da sole (m pl)
sunglasses
occhialini (m pl) goggles
occhio (m) eye

odiare to hate
oggetti di valore (m pl)
valuables
oggi today
ogni each (every)
olio (m) oil
ombrello (m) umbrella
ombrellone da spiaggia
(m) beach umbrella
online online
opaco/a matt
opera (f) opera
ora (f) hour
orario (m) timetable
orario delle visite (m)
visiting hours
orario di apertura (m)
opening hours
ordinare to order
ordine (m) order
orecchio (m) ear
ormeggio (m) mooring
orologio da polso (m)
wrist watch
orribile awful
ospedale (m) hospital
ospite (f/m) guest
otto eight
ottobre October
ovest (m) west

P

pacchetto (m) packet
padella (f) frying pan
padre (m) father
paese (m) country; village
pagare to pay
pagare in contanti
to pay cash
palestra (f) gym
paletta (f) dust pan
palla (f) ball
palla da golf (f) golf ball
palla da tennis (f)
tennis balll
pallone (m) football
(ball)
pallone da spiaggia (m)
beach ball
panetteria (f) baker's

panne: in panne broken (in car)

parabrezza (m) windscreen

paraurti (m) bumper

parcheggiare to park

parcheggio (m) parking

parcheggio per disabili (m) disabled parking

parchimetro (m) parking meter

parco (m) park

parco a tema (m) theme park

parco safari (m) safari park

parlare to speak

parte posteriore (f) back (not front of)

partenze (f pl) departures

partire to depart; to leave

partita (f) match (sport)

pass per lo ski-lift (m) lift pass

passaporto (m) passport

passeggero (m) passenger

passeggiata (f) walk

pasto a bordo (m) flight meal

patente di guida (f) driving licence

patologia cardiaca (f) heart condition

pattumiera (f) dustbin

pedaggio (m) toll

pelle (f) skin

peluche (m) soft toy

penna (f) pen

pensare to think

pensione: in pensione retired

pentola (f) saucepan

per for

per favore please

perché? why?

perdere to lose

perdita (f) leak

persone (f pl) people

pesce (m) fish

pescivendolo (m) fishmonger

pezzo (m) piece

piacere to like

piacevole nice

pianista (m) pianist

piattino (m) saucer; side plate

piatto (m) dish; plate

piazza (f) square (in town)

picchetto (m) tent peg

piccolo/a small; little

picnic (m) picnic

piede (m) foot

pieno/a full

pilates pilates

pilota (m) pilot

PIN (m) PIN

pinne (f pl) flippers

piove to rain

piscina (f) swimming pool

più more

pneumatico (m) tyre

poco little

poggiatesta (m) head rest

poi then

polizia (f) police

poliziotta (f) policewoman

poliziotto (m) policeman

polizza (f) policy

polizza assicurativa (f) insurance policy

pollice (m) thumb

polso (m) wrist

pomata (f) ointment

pomeriggio (m) afternoon

pompa (f) pump

pompiere (m) firefighter

porta (f) door

portafoglio (m) wallet

portamonete (m) purse

portare to carry; da portar via takeaway

portellone (m) hatchback

porticciolo (m) marina

porto (m) harbour

posate (f pl) cutlery

possibile possible

posta post

posta aerea (f) airmail

posteggio dei taxi (m) taxi rank

postino (m) postman

posto (m) place; seat

posto vicino al corridoio (m) aisle seat

posto vicino al finestrino (m) window seat

potere can (verb)

pranzo (m) lunch

preferito/a favourite

prelevare to withdraw (money)

prelievo (m) withdrawal

prendere to take

prenotare to book; reserve

prenotazione (f) reservation

pressione arteriosa elevata (f) high blood pressure

pressione degli pneumatici (f) tyre pressure

presto early; soon

prezzo (m) price

prima di before

primavera (f) spring

primo/a first

principiante (m/f) beginner

prolunga (f) extension lead

pronto/a ready

Pronto Soccorso (m) accident and emergency

prossimo/a next

provare to try

pulito/a clean

Q

qualche volta sometimes

qualcosa anything

qualcosa something

qualcuno/a somebody

quale? which?

quando? when?

quanti/e? how many?

quanto? how much?

quaranta forty

quasi almost

quattordici fourteen

quattro four

quello/a that

questo/a this

qui here

quindici fifteen

R

racchetta da tennis (f) tennis racquet

racchette da sci (f pl) ski poles

radiatore (m) radiator

radio (f) radio

radiografia (f) X-ray

raffreddore (m) cold (illness)

raffreddore da fieno (m) hay fever

ragazzo/a (m/f) boy/girl

rampa per i disabili (f) wheelchair ramp

rapido/a quick

rasoio (m) razor

rasoio elettrico (m) electric razor

reato (m) crime

reclamare to complain

regalo (m) gift; present

rene (m) kidney (medical)

reparto di terapia intensiva (m) intensive care unit

repellente per gli insetti (m) insect repellent

retro (m) back (not front of)

rianimazione (f) resuscitation

riavviare to reboot

ricetta medica (f) prescription

ricevuta (f) bill; receipt

ricevuta dei bagagli (f) reclaim tag

riduzione (f) reduction

riempire to fill

rimorchiare to tow

riparare to fix; repair

riparazione (f) repair

riscaldamento (m) heating

riscaldamento centralizzato (m) central heating

riscuotere to cash

riservare to reserve

ristorante (m) restaurant

ritardo: in ritardo late

ritiro bagagli (m) baggage reclaim

rivelatore di fumo (m) smoke alarm

rivista (f) magazine

rosa pink

rosso/a red

rotatoria (f) roundabout

rotondo/a round

rotto/a broken

rubato/a stolen

rubinetto di arresto (m) stopcock

rullino (m) roll (of film)

ruota (f) tyre; wheel

ruota di scorta (f) spare tyre

rusta (f) whisk

S

sabato Saturday

sabbia (f) sand

sacca da viaggio (f) holdall

sacco a pelo (m) sleeping bag

sala d'attesa (f) waiting room

salute (f) health

salvagente (m) lifebuoy

sandali (m pl) sandals

sangue dal naso (m) nosebleed

sapere to know (a fact)

sapone (m) soap

sarto (m) tailor

sbagliato/a wrong

sbucciatore (m) peeler

scale (f pl) stairs

scarpa (f) shoe

scarpe da ginnastica (f pl) trainers

scarpone (m) boot

scarponi (m pl) walking boots

scarponi da sci (m pl) ski boots

scatola (f) box

scatola dei fusibili (f) fuse box

scatoletta (f) can (noun)

scendere to get off

scheda di memoria (f) memory card

scheggia (f) splinter

schiena (f) back (body)

schiuma da barba (f) shaving foam

sci (m pl) skis

sci (m) skiing

sci d'acqua (m) water-skiing

scodella (f) bowl

scompartimento (m) compartment

scopa (f) brush (cleaning)

scotch (m) adhesive tape

scottatura solare (f) sunburn

scrivania (f) desk

scusi sorry

secchio (m) bucket

secco dry (wine)

secondo/a second

sedia a rotelle (f) wheelchair

sedia a sdraio (f) deck chair

seggiolino (m) child seat

seggiolone (m) high chair

seggiovia (f) chair lift

segnali stradali (m pl) road signs

sei six

semaforo (m) traffic lights

sentire to hear

senza without

senza piombo unleaded

separatamente separately

sera (f) evening

serpente (m) snake

servire to serve

servizi di emergenza (m pl) emergency services

servizio di babysitting (m) babysitting

servizio espresso (m) express service

sette seven

settembre September

settimana (f) week

shampoo (m) shampoo

sì yes

sicuro/a safe

sigaretta (f) cigarette

sinistra left

sito Web (m) website
soggiorno (m) stay
solamente only
soldi (m pl) money
sole (m) sun
solito/a usual
solo/a alone
sopra over
sotto below; beneath
souvenir (m) souvenir
spalla (f) shoulder
spatola (f) spatula
spazzolino da denti (m) toothbrush
specialità (f) speciality
spedire la posta to post
spegnere to turn off
spento/a off
spesso often
spiaggia (f) beach
spina (f) plug
spogliatoio (m) changing room
sport (m) sport
sportello bancomat (m) cash machine
sposato/a married
spray (m) spray
spuntino (m) snack
stagione (f) season
stampa (f) print (photo)
stampare to print
stanza libera (f) vacancy (room)
starnutire to sneeze
stasera tonight
Stati Uniti (m pl) United States
statua (f) statue
stazione (f) railway station
stazione degli autobus (f) bus station
stazione di servizio (f) petrol station
stecca (f) splint
step machine (f) step machine
sterlina (f) sterling
stesso/a same
stitichezza (f) constipation

stivale (m) boot
stomaco (m) stomach
strada (f) road; street; way
stretto tight
studente/studentessa (m/f) student
su on; over; up
succedere to happen
sud (m) south
suo/sua/sue his; her; your
supermercato (m) supermarket
supposte (f pl) suppositories
surfista (m/f) windsurfer
svaligiare to burgle
sveglia telefonica (f) wake-up call
sviluppare to develop (film)

T

tabaccaio (m) tobacconist
tabacco (m) tobacco
tachimetro (m) speedometer
taglia (f) size
tagliaunghie (m) nail clippers
tagliere (m) chopping board
taglio (m) cut
tallone (m) heel
tardi late
tasso di cambio (m) exchange rate
tastiera (f) keyboard
tavola da surf (f) surfboard
tavoletta (f) float
tavolo (m) table
taxi (m) taxi
tazza (f) cup
teatro (m) theatre
teatro dell'opera (m) opera house
teglia da forno (f) baking tray
telecomando (m) remote control
telefonare to telephone
telefonata (f) phone call
telefono (m) telephone

televisore (m) television
televisore a schermo
  panoramico (m)
  widescreen TV
telo da spiaggia (m)
  beach towel
temperatura (f) temperature
tempestoso/a stormy
tempo (m) time
tempo (m) weather
tenda (f) tent
tenda veneziana (f)
  Venetian blind
tennis (m) tennis
tergicristallo (m)
  windscreen wiper
terminal (m) terminal
termostato (m) thermostat
testa (f) head
testimone (m/f) witness
thermos (m) vacuum flask
torace (m) chest
torcia (f) torch
tosse (f) cough
tovagliolo (m) napkin
traghetto (m) ferry
travellers cheque (m)
  traveller's cheque
tre three
treno (m) train
trenta thirty
troppo too
trovare to find
t-shirt (f) t-shirt
tu you
turista (m/f) tourist
tutto/i all
TV satellitare (f) satelliteTV

U, V, Y, Z

ufficio del turismo (m)
  tourist information office
ufficio oggetti smarriti (m)
  lost property
ufficio postale (m) post
  office
ultimo/a last
umido/a humid
undici eleven
unghia (f) nail

uno/a one
uomo (m) man
urgente urgent
usare to use
uscita (f) exit
uscita d'imbarco (f)
  boarding gate
utile useful
vacanza (f) holiday
valigetta (f) briefcase
valigia (f) suitcase
valore (m) value
vedere to see
vegetariano/a vegetarian
vela (f) sailing
veloce fast; quick
vendere to sell
venerdì Friday
venire to come
venti twenty
ventilatore (m) fan
ventoso/a windy
veramente really
verde green
vespa (f) wasp
vetro (m) glass
via (f) street; way
viaggio (m) travel
vicino close (near)
vicino a beside; by; next to
videogioco (m) video game
vidimare to validate
vigneto (m) vineyard
villaggio (m) village
vino (m) wine
violenza carnale (f) rape
visita guidata (f) guided tour
visitatore (m) visitor
viso (m) face
vista (f) view
visto (m) visa
voi you (pl)
volante (f) police car
volere to want
volo (m) flight
yacht (m) yacht
yoga (m) yoga
zaino (m) backpack
zoo (m) zoo

ACKNOWLEDGMENTS

Dorling Kindersley would like to thank the following for their help in the preparation of this book: Elma Aquino and Mandy Earey for design assistance; Nicola Hodgson for editorial assistance; Claire Bowers, Lucy Claxton, and Rose Horridge in the DK Picture Library; Adam Brackenbury, Vânia Cunha, Almudena Diaz, Maria Elia, John Goldsmid, Sonia Pati, Phil Sergeant, and Louise Waller for DTP assistance.

PICTURE CREDITS

Key: a (above); b (below/bottom); c (centre); l (left); r (right); t (top)

Alamy Images: Alvey & Towers Picture Library p111 cb; PhotoSpin, Inc p36 crb; Tetra Images p18;
Courtesy of Renault: p24–25 t;
Getty Images: Reggie Casagrande p146;
PunchStock: Moodboard p6

Jacket images: *Front:* Alamy Images: Martyn Vickery c. *Back:* PunchStock: Digital Archive Japan

All other images © **Dorling Kindersley**
For further information, see: **www.dkimages.com**